P9-DXC-364

do it
YOURSELF
kitchens

Stunning spaces on a shoestring budget

WILEY
John Wiley & Sons, Inc.

CALGARY PUBLIC LIBRARY
NOV   2011

This book is printed on acid-free paper. ♾

Copyright 2011 by Meredith Corporation, Des Moines, IA. All rights reserved.

Published by John Wiley & Sons, Inc., Hoboken, New Jersey
Published simultaneously in Canada.

No part of this publication may be reproduced, stored in a retrieval system, or transmitted in any form or by any means, electronic, mechanical, photocopying, recording, scanning, or otherwise, except as permitted under Section 107 or 108 of the 1976 United States Copyright Act, without either the prior written permission of the Publisher, or authorization through payment of the appropriate per-copy fee to the Copyright Clearance Center, Inc., 222 Rosewood Drive, Danvers, MA 01923, (978) 760-8400, fax (978) 750-4470, or on the web at www.copyright.com. Requests to the Publisher for permission should be addressed to the Permissions Department, John Wiley & Sons, Inc., 111 River Street, Hoboken, NJ 07030, (201)748-6011, fax (201) 748-6008, or online at http://www.wiley.com/go/permissions.

Limit of Liability/Disclaimer of Warranty: While the publisher and author have used their best efforts in preparing this book, they make no representations or warranties with respect to the accuracy or completeness of the contents of this book and specifically disclaim any implied warranties of merchantability or fitness for a particular purpose. No warranty may be created or extended by sales representatives or written sales materials. The advice and strategies contained herein may not be suitable for your situation. You should consult with a professional when appropriate. Neither the publisher nor author shall be liable for any loss of profit or any other commercial damages including but not limited to special, incidental, consequential, or other damages.

For general information on our other products and services or for technical support, please contact our Customer Care Department within the United States at (800) 762-2974, outside the United States at (317) 572-3993 or fax (317) 572-4002.

Wiley also publishes its books in a variety of electronic formats and by print-on-demand. Some content that appears in standard print versions of this book may not be available in other formats. For more information about Wiley products, visit us at www.wiley.com.

Library of Congress Cataloging-in-Publication Data is available on request.

ISBN 978-1-118-03162-9

Printed in the United States of America.

Note to the Readers:
Due to differing conditions, tools, and individual skills, John Wiley & Sons, Inc., assumes no responsibility for any damages, injuries suffered, or losses incurred as a result of following the information published in this book. Before beginning any project, review the instructions carefully, and if any doubts or questions remain, consult local experts or authorities. Because codes and regulations vary greatly, you always should check with authorities to ensure that your project complies with all applicable local codes and regulations. Always read and observe all of the safety precautions provided by manufacturers of any tools, equipment, or supplies, and follow all accepted safety procedures.

MEREDITH CORPORATION

Editorial Director
Gregory H. Kayko
Special Interest Media

Home Content Core Director
Jill Waage

Do-It-Yourselft Magazine Editor
Bethany Kohoutek

**Do-It-Yourself Magazine
Art Director**
Kimberly Metz

Contributing Book Editor
Sandra S. Soria

Contributing Book Designer
Angie Packer

Contributing Book Copy Editor
Elizabeth Sedrel

Books Executive Editor
Larry Erickson

Group Editor
Lacey Howard

Deputy Content Director
Karman Hotchkiss

Art Director, Home Design
Gene Rauch

Administrative Assistant
Heather Knowles

Contributing Designers
Sarah Alba, Kathy Barnes, Bonnie Broten, Meredith Ladik Drumond, Rachel Haugo, Annette Joseph, Stacey Kunstel, Sandra L. Mohlmann, Joetta Moulden, Lisa Mowry, Jean Schissel Norman, Angie Packer, Kathryn Precourt, Wade Sherrer, Stephen Saint-Onge, Donna Talley, Jessica Thomas, Jeni Wright, Kristi S. Zimmeth

Contributing Photographers
Adam Albright, King Au, Marty Baldwin, Kim Cornelison, Paul Dyer, Tria Giovan, Erik Johnson, Keller + Keller, Kritsada, Scott Little, Anthony-Masterson, Bryan McCay, Michael Partenio, Cameron Sadeghpour, Greg Scheidemann, Beth Singer, Jack Thompson, Brie Williams, Jay Wilde

It's easy to feel sentimental about a kitchen—it's where the good stuff happens. First spoonfuls, visits with grandma, family fun ... Whether it's a milestone or an everyday moment, the kitchen is center stage for family life. If yours doesn't seem up to the task, it's time to get cooking with some fresh ideas, do-it-yourself tricks, and solid information. Unlike other kitchen design books, we've created a guide with real families and realistic budgets in mind. Like all of the features in Do It Yourself magazine, these DIY kitchen plans value creativity over cash. To help you picture your own space's potential, the real-life kitchen features that follow come complete with before-and-after photos, detailed budgets, clever shortcuts, and step-by-step instruction for getting the job done, whether that job is a cosmetic perk up or a full-on renovation.

There's more good news. When you improve the style and function of your kitchen, you directly impact the value of your home. Of all the home improvements you make, a kitchen do-over promises one of the highest returns on your investment. So, what are you waiting for?

The kitchen says a mouthful about who you are—as a family, nurturer, host, cook, and maestro of the home arts—make sure yours is as tasteful and inspirational as you dream it can be.

the DIY team

do it YOURSELF kitchens

stunning spaces on a shoestring budget

6 · 40 · 80

Watch for our DIY 101 projects for step-by-step instructions on the following kitchen facelifts:

126

181

makeovers on a

$1,000 budget

8   14   18   24   30

diy tip

Though it looks complex, mosaic tile is easy to install because it is sold on mesh sheets that have multiple tiles evenly spaced and ready to mount. Shop for glass tile when you want a shimmery effect.

a miracle MAKEOVER

It took only two weekends and about $500 to transform this kitchen, part of a former bachelor pad, into an inviting room for cooking and gathering.

"I wanted to play with the design, but I didn't know where to start," says owner Katy Stovall. So she lived with the lack of color, style, and organization for nearly two years, until she had a design breakthrough.

One obstacle was Katy's feeling that she would have to paint the cabinets to add color and definition to the space. Then she came upon a simpler idea: Instead of the hassle of painting all the cabinetry, she opted to ditch the boring white backsplash and replace it with colorful 1-inch mosaic tiles.

To add a modern edge, a warm gray paint replaced the sage green and eggplant purple walls. "The colors are a little unexpected in a kitchen, but I love how they all come together," Katy says. "They fit my style. There's a good mix of neutrals with unexpected pops of color."

What Katy once referred to as her "wine cellar," an awkward dormer space, is now a cozy window seat. "When I first moved in, it had an ugly, uncomfortable cushion on it," she says. "I hated it, so I converted it to a storage area for wine and cookbooks." With the new seat, her cookbooks had to find new designated slots—on two shelves installed to the right of the range now keep cookbooks organized and close at hand, and a narrow cabinet next to the sink was modified to store wine bottles. "I used to just shove random things in it," Katy says of the slender cabinet, "but now it has a purpose."

The kitchen itself also has a higher purpose—to reflect Katy's personal style, classic with a twist of color.

opposite: Resist the urge to use the top of your cabinets as a display area. Adding knicknacks will disrupt the clean line of the cabinet tops, creating a cluttered look—and more for you to clean.

✓ **Budget Breakdown:**

Shelves	$15
Tile backsplash	$229
Drawer pulls	$118
Light fixture	$30
Seat cushion	$50
Paint, supplies	$75
Total:	**$517**

When Katy couldn't find an industrial modern sconce in her price range, she shopped the outdoor lighting aisles of home improvement centers and snagged one in the right style and for the right price, $30.

diy tip

When your kitchen lacks style and focus, turn to the power of paint. Chic, glossy gray defines and highlights a charming dormer in the kitchen. Not often found in a kitchen, the surprising hue is an instant style maker.

the problem
Slanting walls and a lack of color made this kitchen feel choppy and added-on. **the solution:** Tidying up the clutter and adding organized color brought the room into focus on a minimal budget.

Shop for new hardware when you want a quick update. Here, Katy traded in only the drawers' knobs for pulls to gain a sleeker look.

affordable updates
Don't let a tight budget give your style the squeeze.

Install a backsplash. A blend of colorful 1-inch glass tiles replaced the boring white 4-inch porcelain tiles. Mosaic tiles are sold on backing to make installation easy.

Add sneaky storage. Open shelving installed to the right of the range is ideal for cookbooks, The simple shelves made use of an awkward space created by the slanting wall.

Make storage work for you. When a skinny cabinet to the left of the sink had no real purpose, Katy gave it one. She removed the door and used the

shelves to hold one of her simple pleasures: her collection of wine.

Upgrade lighting fixtures. An easy-to-install light fixture in the dormer replaced the original. Browse the outdoor lighting section of home improvement stores, or go the flea market route in search of interesting vintage options.

Add a coat of paint. Painting the walls a neutral gray created a tailored, cohesive feel. It added sophistication and pulled the space together.

how to:
laminate a countertop

In the wrong place for spices and too slim to do much stowing, this cupboard became an instant wine caddy when the door was removed.

Materials:
_Countertop base
_Laminate
_Handheld jigsaw
_Spray adhesive
_Wood spacer sticks
_Laminate roller
_Paste wax
_Laminate trim router with ¼-inch double-flute bit
_File

DIY tips

What makes laminate tricky is that once it's stuck, it's stuck for good. Here are some tips for getting it right before you glue:

_Practice before you tackle your counter. Try your hand at a shelf, or practice using an old hollow-core door as a base.

_Measure twice and cut once. Cut the laminate with a handheld jigsaw, leaving 1 extra inch on each side.

_Use wood spacer sticks to carefully position large laminate sheets before the sprayed surfaces are permanently fused.

What she did...

White appliances, white cupboards, and a white laminate countertop seemed like too much of a good thing, until Katy broke up the sea of white with classic and colorful mosaic tile. Though she chose to keep her easy-to-clean laminate counter, it was lifting in spots and needed some repair. Whether you are replacing or repairing, laminating a countertop is a good project for DIYers with moderate experience. Here's how to do it, step by step.

step 1
Spray and stick. Spray the countertop base and laminate material with contact adhesive. Let dry. Position wood sticks across the countertop. Lay laminate on tops of the sticks with 1-inch overhang on each side.

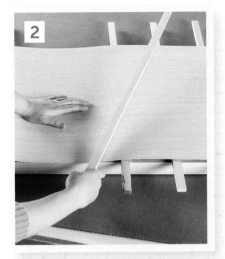

step 2
Remove the spacer sticks. Remove the center spacer stick and press down, smoothing as you press. Continue removing sticks.

step 3
Smooth and roll. Continue smoothing and rolling until all the sticks are removed, applying significant pressure to the laminate roller for a strong bond.

step 4
Slather with paste wax. Rub paste wax on the laminate to prevent the router from burning the laminate.

step 5
Ready to route. Run the router over the laminate edges, working in a clockwise motion.

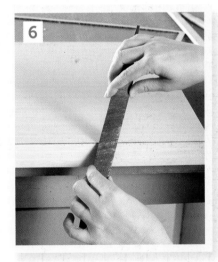

step 6
File to perfection. Finish the edges of your countertop by filing them until they are smooth to the touch.

$1,000 Budget

diy tip

Classic, glazed penny tile brings a sense of timelessness to this kitchen. Use grout in a complementary color to outline and highlight special tile and bring textural interest to the wall.

white
AND BRIGHT

Oak cabinets have always stood for quality and warmth. But after a couple of decades of brown, this family was ready to lighten up.

Brown oak, and a lot of it, was the hottest style goingwhen Rose and Lorne Wazny built their suburban house in the early '90s. They made a lot of other smart choices, too, paying close attention to the details. For instance, they installed solid oak cabinets all the way up to the kitchen ceiling. Rose didn't want to dust the tops of them, and, besides, she knew she'd eventually need the extra storage.

Fast-forward 20 years. The cabinets were still practical, but the yellowed finish now seemed dingy and dated. Once-trendy floral wallpaper wasn't aging well, either. The Waznys were ready for a fresh look. The first and biggest change was painting the cabinets a crisp white. Removing the wallpaper and painting the walls a sunny yellow calmed the room visually and gave it a simple, classic feel. Next to go was the single row of 4-inch-square tile that served as a backsplash. New, glazed penny tiles create a fun focal point, especially with honey-color grout that adds eye-grabbing dimension.

A simple Roman shade made from a cheerful yellow, green, and white lattice-print fabric brings a touch of softness and pattern to the kitchen. The brass ceiling light fixture above the sink was replaced with an industrial-style, antique pewter-finish pendant. The finishing touch was installing satin-nickel knobs and bin pulls to take the place of porcelain and brass knobs on the cabinet doors and drawers.

Now the kitchen is not only brighter, it also appears bigger. Simple upgrades and crisp color invited it into the 21st century.

opposite: The Waznys decided to paint, rather than replace, solid oak cabinetry. The high-quality cabinets were worth saving—and painting them spared the budget.

Budget Breakdown:

✓ Budget Breakdown:	
Wall and cabinet paint	$58
Roman shade	$18
Pendant light	$49
New hardware	$102
Backsplash tile	$208
Total:	**$435**

Sleek, satin-finish nickel hardware adds a classic touch to clean, white cabinetry.

Against a simple Roman shade in lemon and lime colors, a brushed pewter pendant light is silhouetted like utilitarian sculpture.

A penny-tile backsplash adds a nostalgic counterpoint to the fresh white kitchen, as well as enough pattern and texture to draw the eye and hold it there.

the problem

Yellowed oak cupboards and 20-year-old wallpaper dated this '90s kitchen. **the solution:** This couple was hesitant to paint over oak until a designer convinced them they would have no regrets. And they don't.

classic update

Make sure your kitchen makeover is designed to last.

Pick a clean and timeless color palette. Light yellow walls combined with white cabinets to instantly make this room feel larger, brighter, and up-to-date.

Balance white with texture. If you're afraid that too much white will make your kitchen seem cold and sterile, bring in texture to add interesting contrast to the stark, flat white.

Weave in bold fabric. A lattice-print fabric in yellow, green, and white was the inspiration for this update. The Moroccan-influenced pattern adds a modern edge to the classically designed space.

Bring city style to the 'burbs. A metal pendant light is an unexpected urban element. Its simple silhouette blends easily with this couple's clean, understated design style.

Let details tie it all together. New, satin-finished nickel hardware brings out the shine of the existing faucet. Together, the elements echo the steely finish of the new pendant light.

$1,000 Budget

diy tip

If you're working with a tiny space, opt for flooring that's similar in hue to your cabinetry. Maple cabinets pair with light oak flooring to create a seamless look that visually expands the space.

salvage
FRESH STYLE

Don't let a super-tight remodeling budget cramp your kitchen's style.
Shop for salvage materials to stretch your cash and loosen your creativity.

When a bland white kitchen didn't fit with their zesty style, Kate Mattison and Matt Mewis decided to take matters into their own hands.

The first order of business: Open up the cramped space. "Right away, Matt tore out the upper cabinets because they took up so much room in that tiny space," says Kate. "He built and installed the floating shelves on the back wall instead to hold some of our stuff."

A bold swath of orange paint spotlights the couple's sleek white dinnerware and reaches around the corner to help define the space. "I think it's fun to have a bright accent color like that," says Kate, "and because the kitchen is so small, we felt it was a way to give the illusion of a bigger space."

To match the pale woods found in the rest of the house, Matt replaced the counters and cabinetry with materials he discovered at a local Habitat for Humanity ReStore. Though it was the first time he had tackled a kitchen remodel, he dug right in. "I've always been handy," he says, "and I've never been afraid to try something."

Not only does he have the satisfaction of having done it himself, but he also has a good recycling story to share. The cabinets were originally hanging in skyboxes at Atlanta's Philips Arena. Matt stripped the dark woods to their natural finish to keep the space airy. He topped them with gleaming white oak counters that had a former life as a bowling lane.

Clever and colorful accents add to the kitchen's personality. Even the cookware plays along, clad in orange and apple green.

opposite: Kate and Matt's kitchen opens up to the main living area, so they gave it a makeover that matches the modern style found in the rest of the home. Clever recycling and sweat equity kept the budget in check.

✓ Budget Breakdown:	
Cabinets	$50
Cabinet hardware	$45
Countertops	$200
Wall shelves	$50
Backsplash tiles	$30
Jar lighting	$80
Flooring	$300
Paint	$20
Total:	**$775**

the problem

A plain vanilla kitchen with too many space-eating upper cabinets. **the glitch:** A tight budget. **the solution:** This couple got creative with salvaged materials. Plus, they kept the original appliances and did most of the work themselves.

Light kits found at a home improvement store can help you turn any collectible into a light source.

salvage store advice

Tips on where—and how—to dig for salvage treasures.

ReStores. Habitat for Humanity retail outlets, are an excellent source for salvage (and some new!) materials. Builders and home stores donate surplus home improvement items, from furniture to fixtures to flooring, to ReStores daily, so check back often for fresh ideas.

Connect. Get on your local ReStore's e-mail list to stay in the know. Check *habitat.org* for a list of ReStore facilities in 48 states and in Canada.

Dig, dig, dig. Be willing to poke around—some of the best deals are buried. Bring a pair of gloves to spare your hands, a measuring tape and your kitchen's dimensions.

Rise and shine. Visit first thing in the morning to find the best materials.

Go with the flow. "A lot of good things at a ReStore are not necessarily 'remodel-ready,'" Matt says. Keep an open mind, and know that most items can be modified.

diy tip

Short on counter space? Look up! Kate and Matt's kitchen compensates for a lack of horizontal surface area with a high ceiling and plenty of real estate on the walls. Items that might be confined to cupboards—wine, cooking oils, utensils, pots and pans—now double as utilitarian wall decor.

Matt took advantage of space under the stairs to create a niche for the refrigerator. A much-needed pantry is now situated in the corner where the refrigerator once sat.

10 DIY Ideas to Steal

IF THIS 9×9-FOOT KITCHEN COULD TALK, IT WOULD TELL REPURPOSING TALES. IN ANOTHER LIFE, THE COUNTERTOP WAS A BOWLING LANE. THE CABINETS CAME FROM A BASEBALL FIELD, AND THE LIGHTING STARTED AS CANNING JARS. HERE'S HOW KATE AND MATT USED SALVAGE FINDS AND SWEAT EQUITY TO UPDATE THEIR KITCHEN.

1. Open for display

Keep collections tidy on open shelves accented with a color-block backdrop. Create a similar look by masking off a large rectangle with painter's tape (use a level and straightedge to ensure straight lines). Roll on your accent color, remove the tape, and hang your shelves. Matt fastened his floating shelves by first installing brackets and then building a pocket in the shelves to hold the bracket—so there's no outward appearance of how the shelves are supported.

2 Get into the Habitat

Matt and Kate found their cabinets—originally in skyboxes at Atlanta's Philips Arena—at a Habitat for Humanity ReStore for a total of $50. Matt brightened the cabinets by stripping the dark doors to their natural color.

3. Score online

Matt found the bowling lanes at *craigslist.org* (key in "bowling lanes") and used the slabs, which cost $5 a square foot, as countertop material. "I cut them down to size, stripped off the old finish, then called in a favor at a friend's cabinet shop to have them sanded smooth on their flatbed sander. I resealed them with tung oil. It's natural and renewable and food-safe," Matt says.

4 Smart art

The large-scale calendar is from a vintage design that's been around since the '60s. Kate orders the calendars directly from the manufacturer, but she has seen them online at housewares sites.

5. Try old-school lighting

These pendant lights are made from vintage canning jars for retro charm, and the lights are even on a dimmer. A neighbor of Matt and Kate makes them; go to *reclaimedlighting.com*. A local lighting store can create the same look.

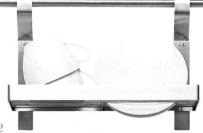

6 Score some storage

Mounted utensil and knife racks place tools close at hand for less than $20. A pot rack and wine rack, both mounted to the walls, make great use of vertical space and reduce clutter on the kitchen countertop.

7. Drawers done right

A small kitchen demands smart storage. Matt reconfigured the cabinet doors to work as drawers because the kitchen didn't have a good place for cutlery and other kitchen basics. Instead of one large cabinet, this space now packs in three hardworking drawers. Divided compartments make the drawers super functional (search for dividers at discount stores).

8 Palette perfection

Too much color can close in a small space. Kate and Matt selected citrus brights as accents to the neutral base (wood flooring and white walls), so they can swap in new tones when the mood strikes.

9. Clean backdrop

Small-scale subway tiles create a clean and simple backsplash. Mounted on a mesh backing, the tiles are easy to install and grout in a weekend.

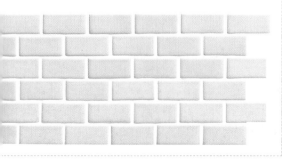

10. Make yearly changes

Kate gives the discount store barstools a fresh look every year by re-covering the seats in a new fabric. She coats the material with a nonaerosol stain repellent for durability. Simply unscrew the seat from the stool, smooth fabric over the seat, staple, and screw the seat back in place. Done in less than an hour!

$1,000 Budget

BURPEE

THE LUCKY FROG

NG for OLD

.59¢

LUCK TEN-FOLD

diy tip

The backsplash in the Gulleys' unfitted kitchen needed to pull the elements together and add some shine. So Melissa bought a roll of roofing aluminum for $10, unfurled it on the driveway, and told her children to hammer away.

creativity
OVER CASH

With just two weeks before her family of four moved in and less than $2,000 to spend, one inventive woman whipped up a cool kitchen.

In her professional life, Melissa Gulley designs living spaces. But in the 150-year-old Victorian farmhouse she and her husband purchased, designing the kitchen had its challenges: time and the budget. "We expected this to be a temporary fix," says Melissa, "so we were budget-conscious and we wanted it to be eco-friendly, too. My husband, Kevin, CEO of Green Collar Economy, is 'Joe Save the Earth.' We wanted to spend our budget on things that were repurposed and recycled and that could be used again later on."

The time and money challenge actually fed Melissa's creative spirit. She refinished the original oak floor, painted the wainscoting bright white, and added firecracker red paint to two walls. "It was screaming for a pop of color," she says.

With a knack for pairing unconventional materials and styles, Melissa pushed inexpensive stainless-steel cabinetry back to back as the base of an island and topped it with thick, refinished floor joists reclaimed from a 200-year-old factory. "Kevin sanded and oiled the boards," Melissa says. "The fact that they were distressed was a bonus—no worries about my kids scratching them."

Though the island offered seating at one end, Melissa added more perches by mounting more floor joists on antique brackets from her basement in front of two windows. Over it, a Katie Trinkle Legge painting the couple purchased years ago echoes Melissa's use of color and shape. "It always makes me smile," she says.

opposite: Melissa came in on time and on budget when creating a happy, comfortable kitchen with repurposed materials. The family loves it so much, the design is staying.

✓ Budget Breakdown:	
Dishwasher	$250
Range	$500
Sink with cabinet	$200
Paint	$70
Hardware	$20
Armoire	$5
Backsplash	$10
Total:	**$1,050**

the problem

The kitchen in this 150-year-old farmhouse was a hodgepodge and needed to be functional fast. **the solution:** Recycled and repurposed materials save money and add personal style.

Inexpensive roofing aluminum becomes an industrial-chic backsplash for about $10.

lean, green design

Tips on where—and how—to dig for salvage treasures.

Frequent salvage shops and thrift stores for materials, accessories, and furniture to decorate your kitchen. Scratch-and-dent sales are also great for snagging a bargain.

Think nontraditionally. Items that are rarely incorporated into kitchens—such as red metal file cabinets—can become focal points.

Remember the power of paint. It's the least expensive way to completely change the look of a room if you wield the brush.

Repurpose an attic or basement item, or invite in accessories such as lamps or wall hangings that would be showstoppers in the kitchen but are merely afterthoughts in other rooms.

Splurge on energy-saving appliances. You might pay more up front, but the long-term savings will be worth it.

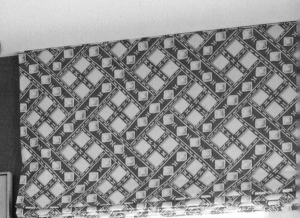

Salvaged floor joists are reinvented as a long, wall-mounted shelf that is used for extra seating and buffet-style service. Installing it mid-window lightens up the look and lifts it to bar height.

Two discount store metal cabinets face off to become an island base. Topping it off are floor joists from an old factory.

This satin cherry red is a happy red that looks good by day and by night. Charcoal and white break up the red and tone down the overall effect.

getting red right

Red gets noticed. Use a lot of red when you want to fire up a dull room. Stick to a shot of red when you need a focal point to grab the eye. A kitchen—the unquestionable heart of a home—is the perfect room to rev up with red. Just be sure it's the right red:

1. Cranberry red has a formal flavor, great for traditional rooms.
2. Fire engine red, like in the Gulley kitchen, is high-energy, kept in check by white wainscoting. **3.** Deep red works like a neutral and blends with many colors, such as pale blue and brown. **4.** Rosy reds show the cool side of red, best for rooms that get a lot of light.
5. Brick red has brown overtones and is a great shade for cupboards.

how to:
sew a roman shade

Roman shades are made from flat fabric panels that fold up, accordion-style, via a simple ring and cord system. Anyone with basic sewing skills can make these tailored shades. Jump-start your shade-making project by reading our general directions. Then purchase a shade-making kit and supplies that meet your style and skill level.

step 1 For an inside mount, measure the width of the window and subtract $^3/_8$ inch to allow for ease of movement. For an outside mount, measure the desired finished width. For either mount, also measure the desired finished length.

step 2 Cut the fabric and lining according to the measurements in Step 1, adding seam allowances to all sides and 3 inches to the total length.

step 3 With right sides facing, sew the lining to the fabric along all edges. Leave an opening for turning. Clip the corners and trim the seam allowances. Turn the panel to the right side, slip-stitch the opening closed, and press the panel.

step 4 Working on the lining side, mark the placement of the pleat lines in the following manner: Starting 2 inches up from the bottom and ending approximately 3 inches down from the top, divide the shade into equal portions for the folds. The normal distance between the fold lines is 6 to 8 inches. Mark the fold lines, making sure they are equidistant, parallel, and straight.

step 5 Pin the shade tape along the markings with the finished edge facing toward the panel top. Check to make sure all the rings are in alignment. Sew the tape strips in place, leaving $1/2$ inch free at either end.

step 6 Slip-stitch the ends of the tape closed. Cut the dowels to fit the tubes and insert them through the bottom insertion slits in the tape.

step 7 Press the loop (soft) side of the hook-and-loop tape to the top edge of the panel. Press the remaining (hook) side of the tape to one of the long, narrow edges of the mounting board. Attach the board to the window frame using screws or L brackets.

step 8 To string the shade, you will run cords through the rings in the tube tape. Start with the ring that is on the bottom row of tube tape and approximately 1 inch from the panel's edge. Tie the cord to the bottom ring and run it through the rings directly above that ring. Repeat on the other side. Divide the remainder of the panel into increments of approximately 10 inches. Run cords at these points.

step 9 Hold the shade to the mounting board and mark the position of the cords. Place screw eyes at the marked points. Install a cleat or pulley according to the package directions.

step 10 Press the panel to the mounting board. Run the cords through the screw eyes and secure them with the cleat or pulley.

Shades without slats at the fold lines and those with a thick fabric base will give a softer pleat than those with a dowel or slat inserted into the fold lines.

Materials:

_54-inch-wide decorator fabric

_Lining fabric

_Matching thread

_Shade tape with rings

_$1/4$-inch-diameter dowel rods

_Hook-and-loop tape

_2×1 board

_L brackets

_Cording/cord pull

_Screw eyes

_Small awning cleat

diy tip

Like many kitchens in older homes, this one has a quirky layout. The stove is separated from the refrigerator by a center peninsula. Calming down the palette and clutter unites the two sides of the space.

little ideas, BIG RESULTS

Update your kitchen without picking up a single power tool using these low-cost, design-conscious ideas.

This kitchen had a lot of the right ingredients: white cabinetry, gleaming wood countertops, the right appliances, cottage wainscoting, and even new four-pane windows. But with the cold and dreary wall color and a mishmash of accessories, the overall look was dark and dated. Enter interior designer Stephen Saint-Onge, with a decorator's bag full of ideas.

Stephen's goals were simple: Lighten the kitchen and make it work harder for a busy family. Simple cosmetic changes, such as a biscuit-hue wall color and classic cabinet hardware, delivered. His advice for getting started is equally simple and sound. "Take stock of what's good in a room," he says, "and then start dealing with the not-so-good. A list of what to change will help you stay focused."

To make the kitchen function more efficiently, Stephen packed open shelves with honey-toned baskets and trays that would keep table linens and dry goods under wraps but close at hand. A small pantry is now tasked with holding (and hiding) the microwave, clearing counter space. Open shelves fill an underused wall to organize more small kitchen items. The accessories that get to stay on the counter share light, white shades. Stove-side necessities are corralled neatly on a tray.

To put the final shine on, artful track lighting and affordable, undercounter strips stream light where it's needed. A schoolhouse-cool pendant light is the final punctuation mark, adding sculpture and ambient light to the sink area.

opposite: Editing design elements to basics such as pottery, wood, wovens, and stainless steel keeps the overall look both refreshingly clean and comfortably warm.

✓ Budget Breakdown:	
Wall paint	$30
Track lighting unit	$199
Cabinet hardware	$65
Pendant light	$17
Faucet	$49
Baskets	$50
Undercabinet lights	$75
Shelving	$48
Bar stools	$120
Glass spray paint	$6
Total:	**$659**

diy tip

Don't let lighting be an afterthought. Do what the pros do and include a lighting plan in your makeover from the start. Include ambient, accent, and task lighting. This schoolhouse pendant offers both ambient and functional light. Track or recessed lighting directs beams where you need them to work.

the problem

A high-contrast color palette and full counters chopped up this small family kitchen. **the solution:** A clean, neutral scheme of wheat and white opens up the space. Baskets add storage and texture.

To add functional light and an artful accent in one swoop, shop home improvement centers for the clean modern lighting.

the clean sweep
Don't start over, just start fresh with these designer tricks.

Lighten the backdrop. Out with the gloomy forest green wall color and in with a neutral wheat tone to complement white trim and cabinetry.

Put clutter under cover. Stephen applied frosted glass spray paint on the panes of the door to the mudroom, hiding a hardworking space.

Keep a low profile. Backless barstools don't create the visual roadblocks that high-backed counter chairs do.

Put style and softness underfoot. Rugs make hardwood floors barefoot-friendly and define work areas. Nonslip rug pads keep them in place.

Add pull-out storage. Matching baskets hold table linens and simplify the overall look of open shelving in the counter peninsula. Nearby, a small pantry gets a reorganization with more lift-and-move baskets filled with spices, baking supplies, and other dry goods.

Color is all around you when you cook—in spices, sauces, and foodstuffs. With such a lively foreground, the paint colors you pick for walls, cabinetry, and other background surfaces become more important. Here, we serve up a few of our favorite kitchen palettes for you to toss into the mix.

how to
choose
your hues

Some of the most forgiving colors to work with, honey tones give virtually any kitchen a fresh but calming start.

palette picks
sweet as honey

Golden drops of color are both warm and bright.

1. Take your cue from the pale golden color of a honeycomb for the largest surface in your room, brushing it on in broad strokes. In a kitchen that gets a lot of natural light, this color takes on a healthy glow. 2. This saturated accent color mimics golden amber, making it a rich, eye-catching choice for trim elements or confined areas where you want a touch of gilt. 3. Lighten up to the color of spun gold on cupboards or backsplashes for a happy, welcoming space. Pair it with crisp white wainscoting, as in the kitchen *above,* for an invigorating backdrop. 4. The mellow warmth of buttercream is always a success. Use it on large areas in your kitchen, and repeat the livable chroma in other rooms of your home.

palette picks
pure and simple

Gather the palest shades of gray, blue, and white for airy style.

1. *Dove gray* is the ultimate neutral, blending easily with most any color. When paired with its color wheel cousins—other whispery shades—the result is a room that has a refreshing airiness and, as a bonus, looks bigger than it is. 2. With a few more drops of black and green to strengthen it, *stone gray* has a strong, structural quality. Use it to set off backsplashes or other secondary surfaces wrought in paler shades. 3. For a scheme as ethereal and relaxing as clouds against sky, as in the kitchen *above,* coat walls or cupboards in soft *cloud blue.* Tinged with drops of black and cool blue, this go-anywhere shade lends a light Swedish touch. 4. Bring out the warmer side of gray with a dollop of *frothy cream.* It's a surprisingly chic duo. 5. Bring a color into focus by surrounding it with *egg white.* Bring in this pure shade on trims and accents to make your other pale shades stand out.

Gray is the easy-to-get-along-with neutral. Shades shift from cool to warm, inspired by one of nature's purest forms.

When your kitchen needs more zest, brighten its spirit with vibrant greens. The dominant hue in nature, green is surprisingly livable.

3

2

1

4

5

citrus squeeze

Add vibrant notes of yellow-green to get that spark back in a kitchen gone stale.

1. Somewhere between the colors found in the flesh of a lime and a stalk of celery is a yellow-green that is as crisp and creamy as *key lime pie*. When played out in sparkling glass tile on the ceiling-to-counter wall *above*, this light and lively shade turns positively effervescent.

2. Pale green—think *young lettuce leaf*—is an all-around favorite decorating hue for its neutrality, especially when paired with silver accents and dark woods. 3. Warm, yellow-tinged *willow green* has a way of refreshing rooms, especially those on the shady side of the house. 4. When you have an element that deserves special attention, paint it a fresh *grass green*. This jewel of a color also looks great as an accent on fabric or glass pieces. 5. It might have been a bad word for a while, but pale *avocado green* is a modern shade, especially when paired with dark green or brown.

palette picks

bold strokes

Use saturated color to highlight your kitchen's best features.

1. Who doesn't enjoy a bit of chocolate? Rich *cocoa brown* is a sophisticated choice for floors, furniture, or accents. Not as strong as black, brown has an earthiness that is easy to live with; you can use it in broad strokes or as an accent. 2. Another go-anywhere neutral is *pewter gray*, a naturally chic shade that blends coolly and calmly with most other colors. Use it on cabinets as an alternative to white, as in the kitchen *above*. 3. Ready to go red? Make it a clear, strong *lipstick red* that is pretty, relatable, and warm. Paired with lighter neutrals, red outlines and sets off other features. 4. When building a palette of strong color, don't leave out blue. A deep *ocean blue* calms other hues, and the room, as only a refreshing water shade can. 5. To set off a strong color, add leavening to the overall scheme. When white is too stark, *creamy tan* will be more warm and welcoming.

Terrace White
53YY 87/070

790C-3
Dolphin

Crisp Linen
19YY 89/040

White High-Hiding RM
98YY 82/022

730C White Cl

ellow
8/180

Autumnal Equinox
10YY 73

Strong neutrals and deep color hint at the lush life. Use them to turn your kitchen into a statement room.

790
Dol

2
3
Spice colors signal warmth, passion, and stability. These savory hues can bring a kitchen to life.
4
1
5

palette picks

savory spice

Glowing spice shades highlight natural wood's warm undertones.

1. As rich and robust as a good cup of cappuccino, a toasty brown is versatile enough to go on trim, cabinets, or walls. It works like a neutral, but with more of a kick. 2. Golden shades bring cheer to a space, especially when pumped up with happy orange. This spiced pumpkin hue is neutral enough to be brushed on medium-size surfaces. Most kitchens have broken wall space; a bold color such as this can lend impact as in the kitchen *above* without being overwhelming. 3. Spice hues can get a bit too hot for comfort. Turn down the heat with a dose of ivory on trim or walls. 4. Sun-baked orange is a clear, clean color that mixes the energy of red with the happiness of yellow. And it beautifully complements a room's wood tones. 5. Use a saturated sunbeam yellow to mimic sunlight in a kitchen that doesn't receive a lot of light.

makeovers on a

$2,500 budget

42 48 54 62 68

$2,500 Budget

diy tip

To gain a designer look on a DIY budget, this couple painted their base cupboards a darker shade than their upper cabinets. Putting a lighter shade on top creates the illusion of a larger, airier space.

dowdy to PARTY-READY

Facing a modest budget and a mishmash kitchen that still had one foot in the '30s only inspired this young do-it-yourself couple.

This kitchen is the epicenter of many parties. Its owners, Brittney and Tyler Rutherford, both work for a large university with its legion of fans, and their first home sits within tailgating distance of the stadium. It's so close that, according to Brittney, "Our parents told us we bought the house for seven weekends a year." The problem was the kitchen wasn't fit for a single party, let alone a season of entertaining.

Afraid of how big a hit a kitchen redo might make on their decorating budget, they waited two years to tackle it. "We always wanted to change it," says Brittney, "but we were afraid of how much money we had to sink into it."

By calling on their DIY skills—and a few handy family members—they created the new kitchen they wanted. The biggest challenge was ripping down part of the wall to the left of the range. They decided while they were scraping off faux-tile wallpaper and a well-worn red linoleum floor that they should eliminate an extra door in the kitchen for more wall space.

Instead of new cabinets, the couple used a coat of paint and new hardware to give the existing ones an update in keeping with the age of the 1930s house. Painted white walls and a white ceramic tile backsplash brightened the space. To balance the white, warm butcher-block countertops replaced laminate ones and earthy tile went down in place of the linoleum.

Adding open shelves on the range wall and around the refrigerator offers both storage and display space. Affordable stainless-steel appliances finished the project in style.

opposite: This 8×13 foot galley kitchen once had little going for it, except its proximity to a popular football stadium. But that was before the Rutherfords dug into it.

Budget Breakdown:

Range	$798
Hood	$229
Faucet	$88
Sink	$99
Backsplash tile	$40
Countertop	$118
Floor tile	$108
Fabric	$60
Hardware/paint	$108
Lumber	$247
Light fixtures	$79
Total:	**$1,974**

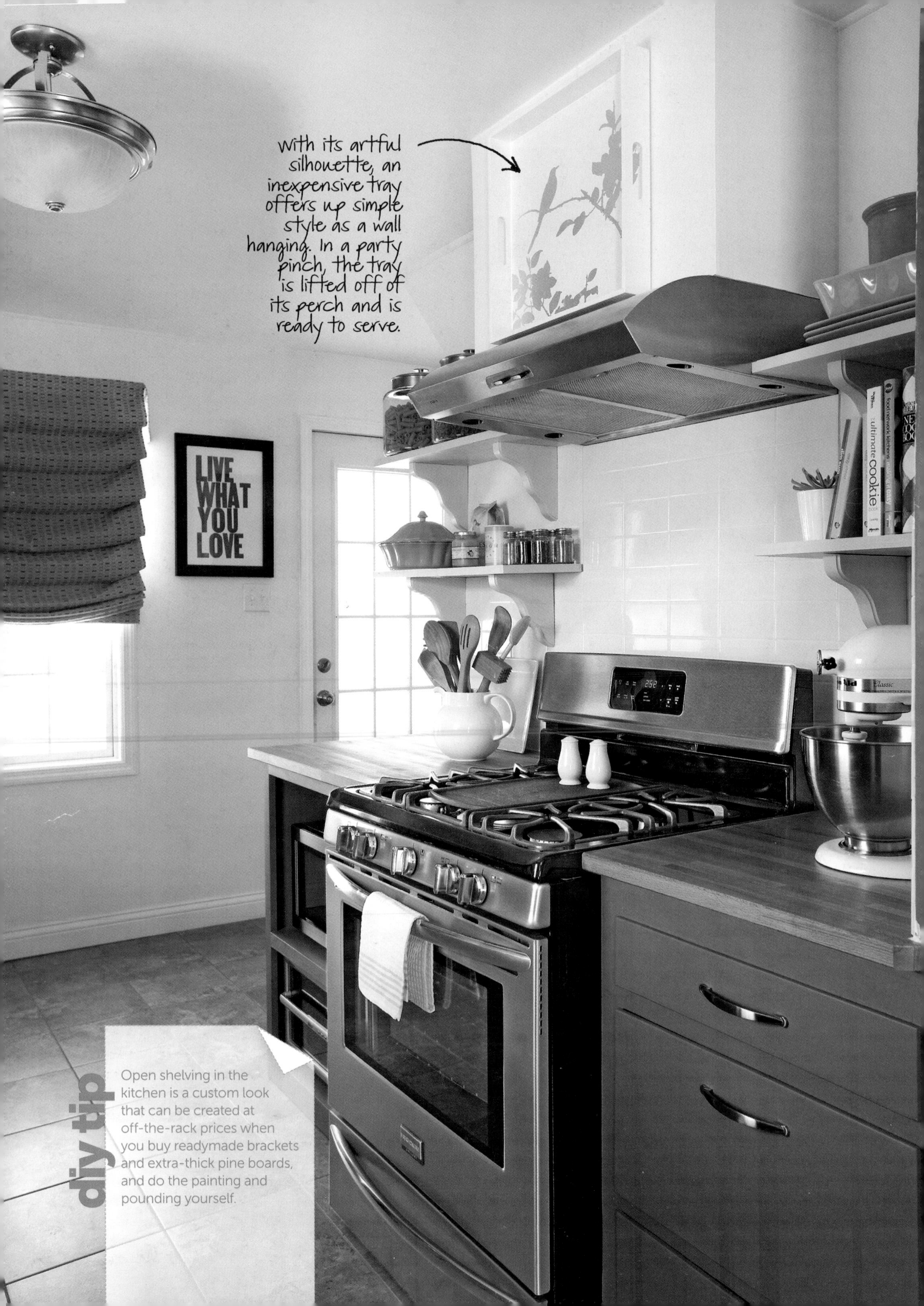

With its artful silhouette, an inexpensive tray offers up simple style as a wall hanging. In a party pinch, the tray is lifted off of its perch and is ready to serve.

LIVE
WHAT
YOU
LOVE

diy tip

Open shelving in the kitchen is a custom look that can be created at off-the-rack prices when you buy readymade brackets and extra-thick pine boards, and do the painting and pounding yourself.

before

the problem

Buying a stainless-steel refrigerator only made the rest of this kitchen more dowdy by comparison.
the solution: Though the owners weren't ready to invest big dollars in a kitchen redo, clever DIY ideas created worthy surroundings for the chic appliance.

The soffit area above the upper cabinets is left open and the interiors are painted a deep gray to look like modern shadowboxes.

pricey looks for less

Tips on where—and how—to dig for salvage treasures.

Open things up. Removing a door and a wall that sealed off a tiny back vestibule gave the kitchen a grander, more spacious feel.

Make room for storage. Removing the door to the left of the range made room for one more base cupboard to finish off the area. The couple purchased a standard stock cupboard and left it doorless to stash a microwave and small wine fridge, *left.*

Tile with style. Classic white subway tile takes on a chic, modern edge when it's installed in a stacked pattern.

Edit the items on display. With mostly white ironstone on view, the kitchen is calmer and more sophisticated than it would be with a mix of shapes and colors.

The look of stone for less. Ceramic tile is great at mimicking pricier natural stone. Select ceramics in natural colors such as this warm, grainy sienna.

Stainless steel gets real. Think professional looking stainless-steel appliances are out of your price range? If you don't really need the cooking power, you can buy the look for less.

4 simple add-ons to do right now

When you want to loosen up your kitchen's style but your budget is tight, start with these personal and price-conscious changes.

1. FILL IN THE GAPS WITH SHELVES. When you find yourself with awkward slices of space, fill them with cut-to-fit shelves that look great and keep your favorite kitchen gear close at hand.

2. SHOP FOR WELL-DESIGNED HARDWARE. New cabinetry costs a fortune, but new hardware can give your cabinets a little facelift for thousands of dollars less. If the hinges work well but look dated, paint them to match the cupboards so they virtually disappear.

3. TURN ON A NEW LOOK. A pendant light has all the impact of that favorite piece of jewelry. Replace dingy lighting, especially where you see it most, such as above the sink.

4. CONSIDER A NEW COUNTER. Countertops take up a lot of visual space in a kitchen, so replacing this surface dramatically changes a kitchen's look. Because it is the easiest material to install, butcher-block countertops are among the least expensive options for a do-it-yourselfer.

how to:
install open shelves

Materials:

_Measuring tape
_Wood Screws
_Hand drill
_Brackets
_Level
_Shelf

DIY tips

To hang heavy shelves, find and place a fastener into a stud. **Studs are usually placed every 16 or 24 inches;** you just have to figure out which interval you're facing!

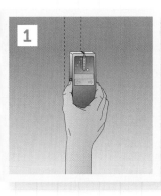

step 1
Finding a stud.
Find a stud by rapping your knuckle on the drywall until you don't hear a hollow sound. Or purchase a special electronic stud finder such as the one here. Find and mark the studs to determine the interval of your house's framing.

step 2
Securing brackets.
Flathead wood screws can be driven flush with or countersunk below the wall surface. Use them to install metal or wood brackets that complement your shelf design. You'll need to place a bracket every 2 to 3 feet of shelf length.

step 3
Keep it level.
A level is your best friend for this project! Once you've located the studs and marked the intervals, use the level to mark and install the remaining brackets. Use the length of your shelf to decide how many brackets you need in total.

What she did...
Open shelves appear to take up less space than upper cabinets, making a small kitchen seem larger than it is but still providing plenty of stowing power. Parade your prettiest everyday ware on open shelves to keep it close at hand.

diy tip

Light trim and walls against ebony-painted cabinetry provide a neutral canvas for dabs of apple green, sky blue, and chili-pepper red. The colorful accents can be changed as trends and color tastes come and go.

black is the
NEW BLACK

This 1950s ranch kitchen needed a color update, but its owners wanted to keep the basic look of the eat-in kitchen intact. See how they transformed their space without resorting to a sledgehammer.

Not all old looks should be experienced again. Tim and Rhonda Leach fell for a 1950s brick ranch and they had to look no further than the cabinetry they called "Werther's yellow" to know it needed an update. "But we really liked the house," Tim says. "The original owner did a good job. It just needed a breath of fresh air"—starting with the kitchen.

The couple sought out a guide for the refresh. They knew what they liked, but meshing their tastes with the parade of designers they brought in to help proved difficult. "Everybody wanted to gut it," Tim says. "We couldn't get through to them that we didn't want to throw away what was original to the house."

Instead, they decided to salvage and update the kitchen cabinets. They had the cabinets sanded and painted a sophisticated matte black, then removed a bulkhead and raised the narrow peninsula to bar height.

Then the couple met designer Jeni Wright. She agreed that the house needed only a consistent, contemporary look to highlight its enduring features. Together, they crafted a uniform design.

Wright built a dining nook with storage-bench seating and a custom table. She accessorized the area with colorful pillows. "I love the way the table and bench help us utilize the space and those windows," Rhonda says. "It's so much more homey than just a table and chairs." To modernize the room, Wright installed new counters and a tiled backsplash. Angled shelving backed by birch-motif wallpaper created a uniform display space.

opposite: The once pale kitchen perks up with a sophisticated black and white color scheme that includes pops of sixties modern art and retro colors that look fresh all over again.

Budget Breakdown:

Countertops	$350
Cabinet hardware	$100
Light fixture	$69
Backsplash tiles	$350
Paint	$200
Labor	$1,000
Misc.	$300
Total:	**$2,369**

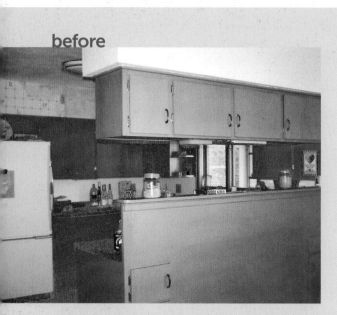

the problem

A bank of bulkhead cabinets needed to go. It closed in the kitchen, visually separating cooking and dining areas. **the solution:** To add seating without gobbling space, designer Jeni Wright created an overhanging countertop supported by brackets. Now, the spot is a bridge between the areas, and makes a perfect perch for lounging with coffee or entertaining guests.

keeping cabinetry

Rethinking cabinets rather than replacing them saves dough.

Start by evaluating the boxes. Are they sturdy? Can they be refinished? Cabinetry is often the most expensive part of a redesign, so take your time and ask a woodworking friend for a second opinion. If your cabinets are solid but dated, you have a few options:

_If the cabinet style is acceptable, consider a minimal paint job. It's easy to do yourself, and you have many color choices when you want a modern, painted look.

_Reface or replace doors on cabinets that are in good structural condition. Go with glass for a more formal look. Or remove doors altogether. Open shelving is a stylish look that you can amend if you find a door style you like later.

_Remove and reinstall. Tearing down bulkhead cabinets, as the Leaches did, can instantly provide a sense of increased space and light. Many times, you can reuse the cabinets for extra storage elsewhere.

diy tip

In small kitchens, getting appliances off counters can seriously improve the surface area situation. Here, a built-in shelf was added to make a niche more functional. It keeps the microwave handy and frees up valuable counter space.

A do-it-yourself table (made by fashioning a circular laminated wood top on a Parsons table base) joins a built-in bench with storage underneath and fun fabrics above. The extra cache keeps clutter to a minimum while linking the eating area to the chic and modern new work area.

6 DIY Ideas to Steal

WANT TO UPDATE YOUR KITCHEN WITHOUT CALLING IN THE CONTRACTORS? TRY THESE FRESH IDEAS TO GET THE LOOK.

1. Go big on a budget

Large artwork can be expensive, but it's easy to make your own. The couple stretched and stapled vibrant vintage-design Marimekko fabric over a piece of MDF (medium-density fiberboard), then framed it in black-painted quarter-inch MDF. Or create your own oversize wall silhouette using black contact paper. Sketch your own design, or print one from your computer. Transfer to contact paper, peel, and stick. Prefer to purchase? *Etsy.com* has a huge variety of ready-to-apply silhouette decals.

3 Bright idea

The Leaches' kitchen needed a statement-making fixture to fill the open space over the breakfast nook and provide task lighting for dining. Big pendants don't have to be pricey; shop discount home stores.

2. Hip hardware

Vintage cabinets often sport hardware in odd sizes. Wright replaced outdated cabinet and drawer pulls with bendable modern hardware that adjusts to fit existing holes. (No need for patching!) New interior hinges further the mod look.

4. Route and roll

The breakfast nook adds function, color, and comfort to the kitchen. Wright built the table on the cheap from two sheets of Baltic birch plywood glued together, with the edge cut in a bevel with a router. The top is sealed with white laminate.

5. Delish decor

Bright colors work well when used sparingly and consistently against a neutral base. The black, tan, and white background is a calm foundation. Too much black in a small kitchen could be overwhelming, so Wright softened the look with a mix of natural textures and shapes. She propped the breakfast nook with pillows, then added plants and even edibles—chili peppers and wasabi peas—as design elements.

6 Tone-on-tone tile

Keep the backsplash the same color as the cabinets to continue a clean, tone-on-tone scheme. Vary the texture for style points without adding a lot of visual noise.

$2,500 Budget

a cosmetic COVER-UP

By tackling the humdrum surfaces in her newly purchased house, this stylista gave her kitchen sparkle and personality on a budget.

The kitchen is America's most renovated room. But sometimes a redo inevitably leads to a much-needed "undo." Such was the case with the galley kitchen in Meredith Ladik's otherwise charming 1939 brick bungalow. "Updated" before it went on the market, the little kitchen suffered from a look more in keeping with a builder-bland first apartment. It simply didn't make sense with the rest of the home's original features and it lacked any hint of personality.

With that disconnect top of mind, reworking the kitchen to reflect its surroundings—as well as its new owner who prefers a feminine look—became the first item on Meredith's punch list once she had settled into her new old house.

The problem she faced—managing a kitchen renovation without tearing up her whole house or spending herself into trouble—disappeared after she hit upon the easiest, least expensive solution: Leave everything in place and more or less resurface the room from head to toe. Armed with pretty paint and wallpaper, plus easy-to-install vinyl floor squares and new tile for the backsplash, this do-it-youself diva set out to glam up her galley kitchen.

She shopped online, at home improvement stores, at antiques shops, and at salvage places, finding her favorite element right away: a broad enamel sink. "I love, love, love the sink," says Meredith. "I know I'm nuts, but the drainboard sink makes me happier than diamond rings."

opposite: Great paint, style-minded surfaces, and loads of imagination are the key ingredients in a tasteful but budget-wise makeover in this standard galley kitchen.

Budget Breakdown:	
Farmhouse sink	$25
Vinyl tile floor	$250
Paint	$175
Countertop	$750
Tile	$200
Wallpaper	$80
Cupboard doors	$400
Faucet	$175
Cupboard knobs	$120
Stock lumber	$200
Total:	**$2,375**

diy tip

For your kitchen redo, consider having your appliances resurfaced instead of tossed out. New panels or inserts or even a pro paint job can give dishwashers and refrigerators a facelift. This is guaranteed to be less expensive than replacing them.

Meredith added unexpected pops of sea-glass green—new glass cabinet fronts and knobs, countertops, even ceiling paint—to boost the kitchen's 1930s feel. Black paint acts like mascara on the lower cabinets, accenting the kitchen's most dominant (and striking) feature.

brace yourself
Easily applied with nails, brackets add instant character.

need to bead
Get an old-fashioned look with beaded trim.

feet first
Give lower cabinets a furniture look with carved wood accents.

go girly
Delicately translucent knobs and handles add instant character.

the problem
White-bread, big-yawn oak cabinets with little charm or detail. **the solution:** Dress up the cabinets with affordable paint, new hardware, stained glass, brackets, and moldings. Punch up other surfaces as well.

simple ways to update your cabinets

Prep for the paint job. Take a deep breath and go for it. Remember, however, that the prep work, including priming, will make or break the project. If you skip these important, albeit tedious, first steps, you won't be happy with the results. Before priming, thoroughly clean the surfaces with a mild detergent to remove any residual grease and grime. Then lightly sand the surfaces.

Prime time. Meredith (and the pros she consulted) recommends using an oil-base primer. Her brand of choice was XIM primer/sealer (*ximbonder.com*). You can use either a synthetic or a natural-bristle brush, but you'll want to have mineral spirits on hand to clean up when you're done.

Fine finish. Though it sounds like overkill, Meredith gave her cupboards four coats of paint on top of the primer. For a smooth final touch, she topped it all with two coats of clear polyurethane.

Haute hardware. This is the easy—and fun—part. Find knobs and pulls that tickle your fancy and simply screw them on. Be sure to find pieces that match up to the existing holes in the doors and drawer fronts. If not, you'll have to drill new holes, fill the old ones, and sand smooth before painting. It's so much easier to find a good match.

More with doors. To bring in an old-fashioned look more in tune with her home's period, Meredith replaced four upper cabinet doors with stained-glass doors that play off the room's new palette.

Easy embellishments. To give these plain-Wayne cabinets more architectural gravitas, Meredith attached inexpensive wood brackets and beaded molding she found at a home-improvement store. She gave the lower cabinets a furniture look by adding painted stock feet and a pedestal center.

Decorative details. As with any project, it's the finishing touches that make a space sing. Here, they all work together to play into the palette Meredith established with the big-anchor black cabinets and green countertop, bold (and fun) wallpaper, stained-glass door inserts, knobs, ceiling paint, and black window trim and curtain rod.

6 tricks for fun and function

Borrow Meredith's clever, cost-conscious ideas:

1. PALETTE. Colored-glass door inserts and matching knobs nearly leap off Meredith's new bright-white palette coating the brackets, beaded trimwork, and mini subway tile.

2. EXTRA SHELVING. Hung below the window as well as over the sink, inexpensive wire shelves offer bonus display space. Add a piece of glass atop the shelf for a super-stable surface.

3. STORAGE. You can never have enough of it, especially in a small galley kitchen. Wire pullouts like these (found at most home centers) make the most of any storage space— and put things in easy reach.

4. TRICKS. Little designer touches don't have to cost a fortune. Meredith replaced two "faux" drawers with ready-made chair caning taped to the inside of the cupboard.

5. FLOORING. Meredith went with vinyl tile in 16×16-inch squares, which are easy to work with. The wicker pattern she chose gives the room some texture underfoot without being distracting.

6 WALLPAPER. Though it's hard to name her new kitchen's best feature, Meredith adores the wallpaper, a last-minute find: "When I saw it, I couldn't believe how perfectly it matched the countertop and the stained glass of the cabinet windows. It's buoyant, bouncy, cheerful, and puts me in a good mood every time I look at it."

how to:
tile a backsplash

Materials:
_ Mastic/mortar
_ Bucket
_ Mixer for mortar
_ Tile sheets
_ Grout
_ Rag & sponge
_ Gloves
_ Grout sealer

Add elegance and function with a gooseneck faucet. Its long neck has a sculptural quality and makes it easy to fill large pots & buckets.

DIY tiling tips

Like painting, laying tile is all about the prep. If you don't **properly prepare the surface,** your work will fail.

Remove wallpaper or paneling and sand painted walls. Or, especially around wet sink areas, **attach cement backer board** for a moisture-resistant and even surface.

Tiling is easy with mesh-backed tile sheets. Plan before applying, however. **Start in the center** and as low as possible, then work out and up. Use scissors to cut the mesh if needed. Go as close to the edges as possible with full tiles and then **fill the space with trim or cut tiles** to abut the edge.

What she did...

One way Meredith improved her builder-grade kitchen was to unify her big, long wall of cabinets. Small-scale, bright-white subway tile adds texture and helps link the newly painted upper cabinets with the lower ones. (The glass inserts, brackets, and trim pieces aid the connection, too.) Now the upper cupboards no longer seem simply stuck on the wall.

step 1

Trowel on mortar. Spread a layer on the wall according to the manufacturer's thickness recommendation. Use the trowel's notched side to draw lines across the adhesive. Work in relatively small sections as most adhesive's workable time frame is 15 minutes.

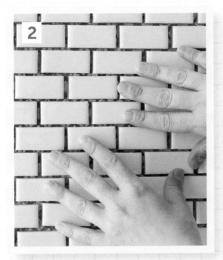

step 2

Adhere to wall. The first sheet is the most critical to place. Get his one straight and the rest will follow. Position, press evenly into place, and apply pressure with your hands for a few minutes. If the tile is thick or heavy, lightly tack brad nails under the top row of tile until the adhesive has cured. To install additional sheets, use plastic tile spacers to keep the tile uniform across the wall.

step 3

Push grout. With a float, spread the grout mixture all across the tile until the spaces are filled. Use the edge of the tool to work grout from the tile surface into the spaces.

step 4

Wash with sponge. Follow the cleanup instructions printed on the grout mix container. In general, cleaning the tile is easy: wipe with a wet sponge until the haze is gone. If desired, seal the grout following the manufacturer's instructions.

TOOL TALK

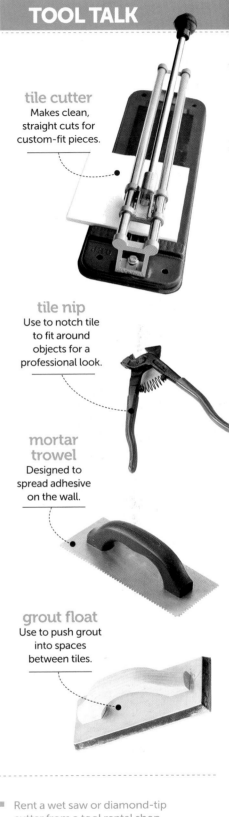

tile cutter
Makes clean, straight cuts for custom-fit pieces.

tile nip
Use to notch tile to fit around objects for a professional look.

mortar trowel
Designed to spread adhesive on the wall.

grout float
Use to push grout into spaces between tiles.

diy tip

Rent a wet saw or diamond-tip cutter from a tool rental shop or home center. These tools are what the pros use, and you'll be able to cut faster and more accurately.

diy tip

Salvaged barnwood
doesn't have to match. Use
distinct pieces to define
activity areas. Note how
wide-planked red, white,
and blue boards announce
the kitchen's entrance and
narrow vertical siding
creates storage.

old stuff, NEW STYLE

TV host and DIY darling Michele Beschen is known for cool and creative recycling. See how she gives new life to old things in her kitchen makeover.

Michele Beschen takes to the airwaves to spread DIY cheer. She's the creator and host of *B. Original,* a program dedicated to hands-on, eco-friendly style projects. So when it was time to redo her family's kitchen, she and her husband, Jon, did it with recycled flair—finding all kinds of budget-happy benefits along the way.

To take some of the pain out of the remodel price tag, Michele kept the framework of her existing cupboards, but replaced the doors with ones made of scrap wood. Refacing rather than replacing cabinets saves an average of 60 percent of a kitchen makeover's cost.

With a little digging in dusty salvage shops, Michele scored two light fixtures, cabinet hinges, and vintage hardware. Hung over the island, the mismatched, under-$100 fixtures make a funky pair. "They add tons of character," says Michele.

To make the floor tiles, Michele cut $^3/_8$-inch slices from a 4×6-inch salvaged wood beam. For grout, she mixed equal parts sawdust and eco-friendly shellac. To further the kitchen's eco-attitude, Michele worked with a team to pour her own sturdy concrete counter. Michele dropped a metal tray into a niche she had cut out of the counter to make a year-round herb garden, complete with a grow-light tucked under the cabinets.

But it's the salvaged surfaces and architectural elements that really wrap this room in chic and unique recycled style. From vintage doors to barnwood to old porch posts, the room cooks with creativity and character.

opposite: Michele kept the cabinet framework, but her kitchen was basically a from-scratch makeover. But that doesn't mean all new! Appliances and surfaces were salvaged from the old kitchen.

✓ Budget Breakdown:	
Concrete counter	$200
Lighting	$70
Door mount kit	$50
Wood floor	$230
Salvaged doors	$570
Faucet	$250
Copper sink	$300
Wall oven	$270
Cooktop	$700
Total:	**$2,640**

6 salvage-savvy ideas

Michele Beschen is known for turning castoffs into cool stuff for her home. Here are a few ideas:

1. CEILING THE DEAL. When Michele's parents mentioned they were tearing down their garage. Michele was first on the scene at the demo. She repurposed the old aluminum siding as a perfectly weathered ceiling for her kitchen.

2. UNHINGED. Traditional swing-open doors eat up 8 to 10 feet in a kitchen. Michele suspended an antique door from rollers on a track to maximize her space. The easy-to-install, wall-mount track was made from a kit she found on the Internet.

3. PANTRY RAID. With no room for a separate pantry, Michele opened one kitchen wall to expose the studs. She decoupaged the unfinished interior with old recipe cards, then added 2×4s cut to size for shelving. Now the nook stores canned garden goodness year-round.

4. FASHION UNDERFOOT. To make the floor tiles, Michele cut $3/8$-inch-inch slices from salvaged 4×6-inch beams. For grout, she mixed eco-friendly shellac and sawdust in a 1:1 ratio. Plywood underlayment keeps the floor level.

5. KNOBBY NEEDS. A vintage doorknob makes an easy-grab handle for a large cupboard. Its bold size catches the eye.

1

2

3

5

4

WEST ST

ELM ST

6 **SECRET SCREEN** Blank TV screens never look pretty—even to TV hosts! So Michele masked hers by gluing vintage street sings to its perimeter. (Be sure to cut space for the controls, if necessary.)

how to:
make a concrete counter

Materials:

_ ¾" melamine
_ Rubber edging
_ ¾" rebar
_ Chicken wire
_ Portland cement
_ Quikrete 5000
_ Penetrating sealer

DIY tips

The materials used to create this poured concrete counter are less expensive than most other countertop picks, such as laminate or stone. But the process for making it requires some DIY know-how. The most important part in the process is to **create a level mold for the poured concrete,** and plenty of reinforcements within it to prevent the concrete from cracking.

Michele added a few decorative touches to her counter. First, she inserted a rubber flower-bed edging material into the mold to create the tumbled edge. She also **troweled in broken bits of recycled wine bottles** and polished it smooth for extra surface sparkle.

step 1

A straight and sturdy mold. Michele and company used ¾-inch melamine with a water-resistant coating. The form was built to accommodate a 2-inch-thick edge, a 1¼-inch counter, and a 1½-inch overhang. Line the outside edge of the form with decorative rubber and glue in place. Michele's was notched to give the tumbled edge effect. Cut out and re-edge areas that will house the sink, faucet, etc., and cover any exposed wood with waterproof tape.

step 2

Reinforce the form. Bend rebar (short for reinforcing bar, a bendable steel bar used to anchor concrete masonry) around cutouts such as the sink and at corners for extra strength. Place one or two bars down the center. Top the rebar with a layer of chicken wire cut to the width of your counter, and secure it to the rebar with steel wire.

step 3

Mix and smooth. Michele used 2 quarts of Portland cement to one 80-pound bag of Quikrete for her special formula, mixed with water. They mixed it with an electric mixer and hauled it in with 5-gallon buckets, troweling the cement smoothly, working from one end of each counter to the other, and being careful to fill in corners and edges. Run an electric palm sander around the form. The vibration will release air bubbles and settle the cement.

step 4

Smooth and shine. After letting the concrete set for five to seven days, it's time to polish it smooth with a wet grinder to the desired effect. After it has completely dried, apply a sealer; finish with a coat of beeswax.

Fabrics with batting add color and softer landings to vintage farm stools. Michele wrapped and stapled the fabric to the underside of the seats.

What she did...

Green glass flecks add sparkle to this concrete counter. To get the effect, Michele hammered green wine bottles to bits. (Wrap them in a towel first!) She placed the shards into her poured concrete counters after they had set for two hours. Then she pressed in the glass further with a trowel, smoothing as she went. After drying, the glass is polished smooth.

$2,500 Budget

diy tip

A straightforward cart on casters serves up more work and storage space wherever you want it. Its tin "belly" band ties the piece to the stainless-steel appliances. Shop restaurant supply stores for similar styles.

white
WARMS UP

Using clever, do-it-yourself upgrades, Nico and Kristin van Praag added personality and efficiency to their basic white kitchen.

A little black dress is essential for a night out, but it isn't a head-turner without the right accessories. That's how this couple felt about their kitchen in their newly built home. "It was 80 percent done," says Nico. Beaded-board cabinets, sleek black counters, and stainless-steel appliances were great, but the kitchen had no millwork, minimal lighting, and little storage.

Enter Nico's handyman skills. Because the priority was more storage, a little-used closet was the first to get a makeover, becoming a hardworking pantry. Nico ripped out the closet's linoleum floor and installed classic penny tile. He considered designing and building a shelving system before discovering that a closet company's work was more cost-effective. Nico used his own handiwork to make a custom wine rack to fit.

New baseboards connect the pantry to the rest of the kitchen, which didn't have any trimwork when the Van Praags moved in. "I started from the floor and worked my way up," Nico says. For more texture and finishing, Nico added new mosaic tile to the drywall backsplash.

To add personality and pop to the white kitchen, the Van Praags layered on vintage pieces. The copper pendant over the sink was snagged at a flea market. The artful iron light fixture in the adjoining dining room started as an oil lamp in Nico's boyhood home in Holland. He wired it for daily use. The light and airy space relies on these special pieces, plus a framed view of the backyard to add the right amount of color.

opposite: Mellow wood floors, stainless-steel appliances, dark countertops, and a copper pendant light add the warmth of contrast to the Van Praags' white kitchen.

✓ Budget Breakdown:

Cabinetry	$300
Faucet	$100
Sink	$250
Light fixtures	$30
Backsplash	$1,000
Paint & supplies	$50
Pantry tile floor	$750
Molding	$75
Total:	**$2,555**

diy tip

Dark counters add definition to a mostly white kitchen the way eyeliner does for eyes. For more contrast and utility, add a butcher-block section next to the stove. Nico made this one out of scraps from a previous project.

Little touches of personality instantly make a new house home. Nico electrified this family antique. No family light legacy? Shop at antiques stores specializing in lighting for the best deals and selection.

affordable add-ons

Add personality to a new kitchen the do-it-yourself way.

Add only what you need. New upper cabinet doors with glass fronts add sparkle to the kitchen, as well as needed dish storage by the sink.

Finish an underused closet. Nico found an affordable closet system to convert a plain closet to an easily organized pantry. He added simple textured glass to the door and finished the floor with penny tile.

Upgrade fixtures. A new porcelain sink and fixtures in standard configurations made the sink a better fit without a big investment.

Do your research. Before you start any project, check out design magazines, books, retail stores, and websites for ideas you can adopt. Take your time during this phase of the project to save frustration and guarantee you'll like your work in the end.

Don't underestimate your skills. Installing baseboards or moldings doesn't require expert carpentry skills. Invest in a miter box and your work is made easier.

how to:
install a pendant light

An antique copper fixture, plus glittering glass shelves, mosaic tile and crisp white trim, give this window a brighter outlook.

Tools you need to have on hand:
_Level
_Screwdriver
_Wire stripper
_Power drill

DIY tips
Electricity should be handled with care for obvious reasons. Follow this safety checklist:

_Flip off the circuit.
The circuit breaker is in a metal box mounted on the wall in your basement or garage and should be labeled by room.

_Double-check the light. The most important thing to remember with this project: Test the existing light and make sure the power is off.

_Call an electrician.
If your old light hasn't been working right, or you see frayed wires, call in a pro.

Light it up in less than an hour.
Put some fresh shine in your work area with a dangling pendant light. Most pendants are basic fixtures that have simple wirings: a black wire and a white wire. Depending on the age of your home's wiring, there might be an exposed copper wire or a copper wire covered with a green sheath. If the box was wired for a fan, there might also be a red wire. When you put up your new fixture, match the wires from the ceiling to the wires in the fixture. Too many wires in your ceiling, or frayed wires, mean it's time to call an electrician.

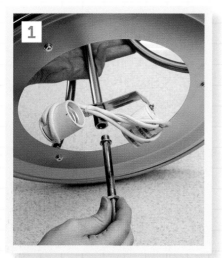

step 1
Know the pieces. The fixture shown here has a short threaded pipe called a bushing in the middle of the base. Because pendant lights drop from the ceiling, there's also a threaded pipe extension called a nipple. Screw the nipple into the bushing. (Depending on the fixture you choose, steps and pieces might vary.)

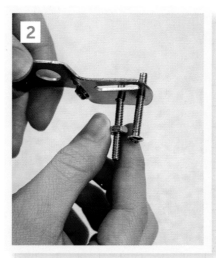

step 2
Thread the mounting bracket. Fixture screws included in the new light should be threaded through a mounting bracket as shown here. Thread the hex nuts onto the fixture screws, but do not tighten the hex nuts yet.

step 3
Attach the mounting bracket. Screw the light fixture mounting bracket to the outlet box in your ceiling. It's helpful to call in a partner before the next step to support the fixture while you wire.

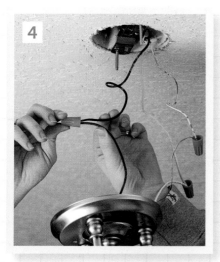

step 4
Wire it together. Link the wires from the ceiling box to the light fixture with wire connectors (they look like small plastic caps, as shown). Be sure to connect black to black, white to white, and copper to copper. Check that the connection is secure by tugging lightly on the wires.

step 5
Tuck it all in. Carefully tuck all wires into the outlet box and place the fixture's canopy over the box. Now tighten the hex nuts; the fixture screws should protrude through the holes of the canopy about ¼ inch. Secure the canopy to the outlet box using thumb nuts. Screw lightbulbs with the proper wattage into the lamp socket.

step 6
Put it under glass. Place the glass shade and then the rubber washer over the nipple. Finally, screw the hex nut onto the nipple and attach the finial.

how to
make a
splash

Replacing a kitchen backsplash is a big deal. Dressing it up a bit—not so much. Check out these easy ideas to turn a tired backsplash into a fashion-forward style element. They'll tickle your eyes and make your budget happy, too.

Crisp white beaded-board adds texture without the busyness of pattern.

splash of style
sticky notes

Decals designed to adhere to tile add style in an instant.

Complete with self-adhesive backing, these peel-and-stick decals, *opposite,* go on easily and peel right off when you're ready for a change. Shop for decals online or at a kitchen shop. Chose a simple design that pulls color from the rest of the room so the new motif will blend in, and not appear to be an afterthought. Apply the decals in a random pattern for a casual look or in a uniform pattern when you want to enhance a traditional design. Look for decals that are washable and water- and heat-resistant.

splash of style
cottage charm

Beaded-board paneling is easier to install than tile.

Put your grout and putty knife away. Beaded-board paneling, *above,* is easier than tile to cut, affix, and, in most cases, afford. Sold as panels, this charming material can be cut to fit with a jigsaw or circular saw. Buy unfinished beaded board and brush it the color of your choice with glossy paint for a washable finish. Butt it up to the cabinet edges and top any unfinished edges with simple moldings that play along with the paneling's cottage simplicity.

No grout is needed when you use this tumbled-stone panel as a backsplash.

splash of style
rock on

Prestacked stone panels add natural beauty.

Natural stone veneers have been used for years on fireplaces and accent walls. So why not bring their rustic elegance to the kitchen? Prestacked in sections (ours, *opposite,* are 24×6 inches), the stone panels are affixed to walls with good-quality tile adhesive. No grout is needed, but the stone should be sealed against moisture.

splash of style
plexi power

Encase pretty papers in acrylic plastic for personality.

A bit of delicate pattern, *above,* can be just what a kitchen needs. When you can't find the right wallpaper, encase a pretty handmade paper behind a waterproof shield of acrylic plastic such as Plexiglas that's been cut to fit at the home store. First install the paper, then mount the acrylic panel using mirror clips.

splash of style
picture this
Photo ledges let you get personal in the kitchen.

When the look of your backsplash falls flat, install a barely-there picture ledge, *above*, to hold your favorite plates or artwork. Installed directly onto tile with construction-grade adhesive, this stainless-steel version underscores the kitchen's modern look. But there are many styles and finishes of ledges available to highlight your style.

splash of style
stick to a script
You'll want to see this writing on the wall.

Texting behind the wheel is a bad idea, but text on walls is great way to say what's on your mind. Found online and at crafts stores, vinyl lettering, *opposite,* is available in predesigned or custom phrasing. The lettering comes on transfer paper that you simply rub onto the wall using a plastic scraper. Just peel it off when you have a fresh message to share.

Save room for dessert

makeovers on a

$5,000 budget

82   88   94   100   108   114

diy tip

Search rooms and storage areas for pieces to refurbish. The island in the Maready kitchen spent some years in the basement, until Wendy decided a soapstone top and a hint of blue paint would invite it into the new plan.

big savings, BIG STYLE

Hurricane Isabel pushed up the plans for this remodel when she left this North Carolina home standing, but soaked. In the aftermath, a fresh style emerged.

"We had to redo the entire inside," says homeowner Wendy Maready. She and her husband, Keith, salvaged what they could and replaced the rest with smart shopping and their own labor. First on their list: the kitchen and dining room.

The couple traded in their kitchen and dining room's worn-out, dated country style for a chic but casual seaside cottage look that was easy on the pocketbook. Wendy estimates the remodel took six months from planning to completion. "It always seems like a major undertaking, especially if you want to watch your costs," she says, "but I found lots of ideas by browsing through magazines, surfing the Internet, and visiting flea markets."

Wendy and Keith liked the layout and essential elements of the kitchen, which yielded them serious savings from the start. No plumbing or electrical changes were required. Formerly dark wood, the cabinets just needed an update with sparkly new doors. The windows and walls also stayed put. Even the appliances hummed along, with utilitarian white and stainless-steel surfaces that would easily shift to the fresh cottage look Wendy had in mind.

A few splurges and a lot of cost-saving ideas balanced the Mareadys' budget and yielded a cottage style that matches the fresh-air feeling of the ocean, only steps away.

opposite: A marble countertop, beaded-board ceiling, and custom cabinet doors are the big-ticket items in this kitchen. New paint, light fixtures, and floors complete the makeover.

✓ **Budget Breakdown:**

Beaded-board doors	$500
Glass-front doors	$450
Hardware	$100
Light fixtures	$535
Beaded-board ceiling	$500
Countertop	$980
Flooring	$1,000
Soapstone for island	$150
Paint	$250
Total:	**$4,465**

6 cost-saving tips

The Mareadys' strategies can be adapted to any kitchen update. Take note of these:

1. SPLURGE WHERE IT COUNTS. In place of laminate counters, carrara marble adds subtle cool to the room. Installing it themselves saved Wendy and Keith money. Covering standard ceilings with porch-friendly beaded-board paneling reinforces the informal feel.

2. SHOP SMART FOR STYLE. The couple chose affordable laminate flooring with a convincing dark-wood pattern. "It's easy to keep clean even with the sand from the beach," Wendy says. The same home improvement store yielded eye-grabbing light fixtures.

3. TURN ON A NEW LOOK. New cupboard doors in glass and beaded-board had to be custom-made, which was still less expensive—and disruptive—than replacing the framework.

4. KEEP WHAT YOU CAN. Appliances in white and stainless-steel have a timeless simplicity. When it came time to lighten their kitchen's look, the Mareadys were happy they invested in well-made, classically styled pieces.

5. SHOP SMART OR SCAVENGE. An island table was rescued from the basement and restyled into a focal-point island with flea market soapstone on the top. "The bottle opener was my grandfather's," says Wendy. "I used it all the time as a kid."

6. BRIGHTEN ADJOINING ROOMS. Reupholstered dining chairs found for a song at a flea market, a vintage farm table that was requisitioned from elsewhere in the house, and breezy ready-made sheers on stainless-steel rods lift the dining room's mood. Those items, plus the whisper-blue paint, refreshed this often-used room for less than $800.

6

diy tip

Wendy tapped the talents of good friends Ann Nicholson, a design pro, and Deborah Nash for interior design feedback. Deborah makes and sells the artful seashell mirrors in Bogue Sound, North Carolina.

how to install:
laminate flooring

Materials:

_Underlayment (one roll covers approximately 100 square feet)

_Utility knife

_Laminate flooring (glueless installation)

_Circular saw or handsaw

_Sawhorses, one pair

_Clamps

_Installation kit

_Jamb saw

_Hammer

_Tapping block

DIY tips

Let flooring sit in the room for at least 48 hours. This allows it to adjust (by expanding or contracting) to the temp and humidity to avoid buckling later.

Remove existing trim. Use a pry bar to remove baseboard, setting pieces aside.

Plan the layout. Determine which way to orient the planks. Start with the longest, straightest wall and run planks parallel to it.

The homeowners saved hundreds by selecting laminate flooring they could install themselves from a kit.

What they did...

Fool-the-eye laminate flooring gleams like rich brown oak, stoking some warm contrast to the pale, cool blue and white scheme. Laminate flooring is found at home improvement and specialty stores, often in a kit. It's a beautiful way for homeowners with average DIY skills to step up their homes' style.

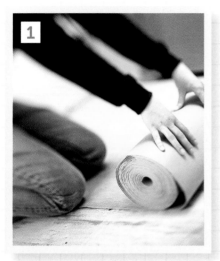

step 1

Install foam underlayment.
Floating laminate planks should be instaled over a hard, smooth surface, such as laminate or plywood subfloor. Cut pieces with utility knife to fit, without overlapping strips.

step 2

Cut the first row of laminate.
Depending on your layout, you may need to rip, or cut, the first row of planks lengthwise. If using a power saw, cut with the finished side down; if using a handsaw, cut with the finished side up. Use clamps to steady the planks.

step 3

Leave an expansion gap. Wedge the floor kit's spacer chips between the wall and the planks to leave ¼ inch for pieces to expand and contract.

step 4

Install the first row. Install the planks with the tongue edge facing the wall. When you get to a door casing, cut the casing ¹/₁₆ inch from the top of the subfloor with a jamb saw, enough room for the laminate plank to slide under it.

step 5

Connect the planks. Snap one piece to another by connecting the tonges and grooves. Fit them by hand or use a tapping block and a hammer to secure the strips.

step 6

Install additional rows. As you snap on new rows, stagger the seams at least 12 inches from adjoining rows. You can often start a new row with the rest of the plank you cut to end the previous row. Slide the last row in at an angle, using a pry bar to gently place it. Leave a ¼-inch expansion gap between the last row and the wall.

diy tip

Affordable cabinetry encases a new stainless-steel refrigerator to give it a bulit-in look. White laminate cabinetry and counters separate and define graphic patterns and poppin' fresh color.

color it
REFRESHING

This design expert gave her pale peach kitchen a healthy dose of bright color. Cheery hues and graphic patterns put a happy face on the tiny cooking space.

This postmodern, 1958 condo boasts clean, open spaces and a wall of glass that scoops up light and a treetop view of an expansive city park. That's why Jessica Thomas, an art director of photography and design, fell in love with it at first sight. What she wasn't mad for was the timid palette, especially the lifeless pale peach kitchen. Bye-bye it went, replaced by saturated color, striking patterns, and streamlined furnishings for a sophisticated look she describes as "upbeat and layered, with interesting moments to discover in the details."

Jessica starts with a pumped-up palette of yellow and blue, with shots of hot pink. She pulls the expressive hues through her home in accent walls and accessories, balancing them with generous amounts of black and white. "I wanted my rooms to be bright and have emotional impact," says Jessica, "making my guests and me smile when we walk in the room."

The dented metal cupboards in the kitchen were an easy toss. Most of the top cabinets were replaced with white open shelves and an aqua backdrop that promote Jessica's 1970s dishware collection. Jessica replaced the original appliances with up-to-date energy-saving models. For a more balanced food-prep space, the appliances were shuffled to make room for a new sink and cabinet in the center of the action. To give a semblance of a wall that finishes off the space, Jessica scooted in a ready-to-assemble pantry cabinet beside the fridge. The white cabinets and countertops leaven the color and lighten the mood of the space.

opposite: Marble floors are just one of the perks of this midcentury-built condominium. Layering fun and friendly shapes, colors, and accessories melts away the formality of the material, leaving a great-looking, yummy-feeling floor.

✓ Budget Breakdown:	
Cabinets	$1,800
Hardware	$150
Countertops	$450
Wall shelves	$50
Flooring	$300
Shelf brackets	$60
Refrigerator	$1,200
Range	$800
Sink	$200
Total:	**$5,010**

before

the problem

This slender kitchen is open to the main living area. Its neutral tones didn't jibe with Jessica's love of saturated color. **the solution:** She chose a bold palette.

Jessica's design DNA

This expert shares her secrets for photo-perfect style.

Break the rules. Choose fabrics, colors, and accessories that make you happy—just maintain a limited and cohesive palette.

Experiment a little. Go bold with color in paint and accessories, such as art and pottery. Live with the change to let your eye adjust; redo it if you don't feel satisfied after a couple of weeks.

Give style a warm boost. Layer in shapely glassware,

fresh flowers, and plant life for natural warmth.

Arrange lively still lifes. Shelves and empty counters are like pedestals for displaying collections. Make yours more dynamic by layering heights and shapes.

Shop for cool function. Even mixing bowls and wall clocks should be bright and well designed.

Jessica's collection of
Iittalia Scandinavian
glass—loved for its
clean, organic shapes—
influenced her lighting
choice here, which
is highlighted against
the sea of blue. The
chandelier was a find
from an architectural
salvage shop.

Jessica carried the blue
hue from kitchen to
eating area, painting
cupboards and partial
walls . The contained
shots of color brighten
but don't overpower the
spaces, especially when
balanced with plenty of
white and black.

10 DIY Ideas to Steal

WANT TO SPLASH YOUR KITCHEN WITH COLOR? GET THIS BRIGHT, MODERN LOOK WITH THESE AFFORDABLE ADD-ONS.

1. Laminate cures

For a clean, modern look, bright white laminate countertops in a matte finish and with square edges blend with the simple lines of the new cabinets and shelves. New tops not in your budget? Revive old counters with a water-base paint and polyurethane sealant that's food-safe. Or try a one-step product sold as "countertop coating." Paint updates laminate cabinet fronts, too. Like a shot of Botox, an energetic blue paint was an instant age-eraser for this side of the peninsula.

2. Tap into the home team

Can't afford a private kitchen designer? Architects and certified designers who know product lines inside and out often staff kitchen sales and design desks at home centers. Such services are our favorite word—free.

3. Secret stash

Jessica's peninsula came with a drop-down bar cabinet on the end—perfect for entertaining. To adapt a cabinet door, look for specialty hinges.

4. Mod hardware

Decorative hardware companies offer hunky versions of their cabinet drawer pulls for use on built-in appliance doors. A 12-inch appliance pull adds a balanced look to the tall pantry door (and makes it easier to open), and is a companion to the standard 3-inch pulls used throughout the kitchen.

5. Organize for efficiency

Outfit base cabinets with easy-to-install organizers—most install using just a drill and driver. A new pullout wire rack keeps pots and bowls easy- access and organized, and a pull-out recycling unit keeps garbage out of sight.

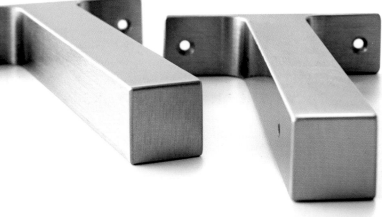

Easy elbowroom

A galley kitchen can easily feel cramped. Add elbowroom without tearing out walls by trading upper cabinets for open shelving. Here, barely-there metal brackets suspend $5/4$-inch hardwood boards purchased at a lumberyard. Because they support the heavy load of dinnerware and books, the brackets were fastened to wall studs for stability and safety.

Smaller is smarter

Though slimmer than a full-size fridge—it's 24 inches wide versus the 36-inch girth of a traditional unit—a small refrigerator can make up for lost space with an efficient interior plan. Three freezer drawers act like file drawers, keeping frozen foods organized and easy to locate. And at counter-depth, the fridge maintains a lean look.

9. Pantry with a pullout

Who says a pantry has to have four walls? Here, a standard-size pantry cabinet unit with pullout shelves shoulders up against the fridge. Inside, baskets and plastic bins organize spices and baking supplies; built-in handles make them easy to tote to the counter.

7. Tile as wainscoting

European homes abound with tile installed as paneling. With their low-sheen glaze and stylized basket-weave appearance, the tiles add texture and artistic flair, often for about $3 per square foot.

10

Put on a happy hue

Jessica chose a bright aqua paint, inspired by her Finnish glass collection, for kitchen walls and some base cabinets because it makes a major design statement.

$5,000 Budget

sweet and
CREAMY

Using a café au lait palette, resourceful redos, and a simple, functional layout, this young family reinvents farmhouse chic for today.

A makeover left this kitchen much improved, but not necessarily new. In their Greenville, South Carolina home, Maria Garuti and husband Bill Humphrey salvaged what they could before taking to the hunt for bargain and secondhand appliances and accents.

Happily, upper cabinets were in good shape, needing only new doors. The sturdy center island also got an update, with a creamy coat of paint, beaded board, and a new butcher-block top. The couple stayed within the L-shape of the original kitchen, sidestepping the cost of moving plumbing or wiring. They picked up a range from a friend who had upgraded her appliances, and the dishwasher was a Craigslist steal. Those savings bought them a new refrigerator and base cabinets.

More online shopping successes include the apron-front sink and the vintage tin tiles Maria snipped to create a backsplash. Even a stroke of bad luck turned into a budget plus. "My best find was also one I got burned on," she says. When she ordered a nickel faucet that retails for more than $1,000 for "a ridiculous deal" at only $250, the handy couple realized it had a crack in the neck the minute it was installed. Resourceful Maria went back to the source. "The person I bought it from refunded us $50," she says "and I ordered a new neck for $250. So it was still a good deal. That faucet makes a statement."

Shopping skills and DIY talents mean more in their wallet and a sense of pride. "We use the spaces we imagined and created for us and our son, Noah," she says. "It's rewarding."

opposite: Soft color on walls, ceiling, and molding visually connects the kitchen and adjacent breakfast nook. The chandelier is an aged brass piece Maria painted blue-gray for subtlety.

✓ Budget Breakdown:

Dishwasher	$175
Refrigerator	$1,400
Cabinets	$700
Hardware	$200
Faucet	$450
Sink	$398
Tin backsplash	$50
Beaded board	$200
Countertops	$395
Lighting	$160
Paint	$200
Total:	**$4,328**

One upper door
and one lower door
were coated with
chalkboard paint
for interactive fun.

what:
tea
cereal
butter
milk
cranberries
cream

Replacing solid upper cabinet doors with paned glass adds sparkle. Maria painted the insides taupe to link them to the island.

Old farmhouse sinks are often deeper than today's standard counters. Fashion a simple shirred skirt to even things out.

tips and tricks

Try this couple's DIY-friendly ideas to personalize your kitchen and stay on budget.

Think about the big picture. Flip through books, magazines, and websites, marking items you like. You'll get a good idea of how they'll look in your space by seeing them in the context of the whole setting.

Sprinkle in vintage textures and pieces. Not only can you snag a bargain on salvaged goods, but you'll send out a gracious message to visitors. "I think people feel a sense of warmth when a space isn't too shiny or new," says Maria. "They pull up a stool and feel at home."

Age with paint. New lower cabinets were painted white, then given a light sanding for an always-been-there feeling.

Toss in a few surprises. A midcentury-modern table is unexpected in this country kitchen, which personalizes the room and updates the whole scheme.

Arrange pretty and personal vignettes. A shelf installed in front of the sink window lets the couple display favorite pieces and seasonal decorating. The salvaged window above the shelf adds another layer of interest.

Reinvent pieces with new coverings. The kitchen island was standard order, until the couple got busy repanelling the sides and giving it an old-fashioned butcher block top. This saved them thousands over replacing the piece.

An island could be just what you need to direct traffic, add storage, and offer more counter space for prepping and serving. In this kitchen, stools are pulled up to the short end of the island to let observers watch while staying out of the cook's work area, in the crook of the L.

how to:
plan the perfect layout

No matter what shape or size kitchen you have, the right configuration will give you elbowroom and save you steps. Here are some tried-and-true tips to consider as you sketch out your kitchen plan.

Try on a triangle. Beginning way back in the 1950s, a concept called the work triangle guided kitchen layouts. But that was back when Mom was solely in charge of meals. Now more cooks in the kitchen means creating triangle isn't always the point. Still, the basic idea of the triangle lives on: Imagine lines drawn between the sink, range, and fridge. If this works with your kitchen and your lifestyle, use it as a guide.

Consider space. As you're measuring the space you have available, keep your main appliances in mind. If any leg measures less than 4 feet, the area feels cramped. If it's more than 9 feet, the cook wastes steps.

Create an island. If space allows, an island works well for how we cook today. An island allows two or more people to work, while facing each other. It also makes a ready spot for fast, casual meals. Install a cooktop or a sink in the island, and you've created more room to prepare meals in the same footprint.

L-shape with island With workstations on two walls, this plan adds an island. The plan works best in a 10x10-foot or larger room. It makes space for a second cook and routes traffic out of the L's crook.

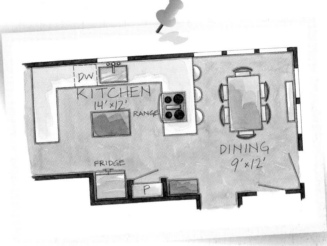

two-wall galley Parallel walls create a compact plan that lets the cook move easily among workstations. Ideally, there should be 4 feet of space between counters. A peninsula can help create a more efficient triangle.

U-shape with island Do you have room for an island? You do if you can have 42 inches of aisle space on all sides of it. Island plans are less efficient when workstations are on opposite walls, but this configuration works well.

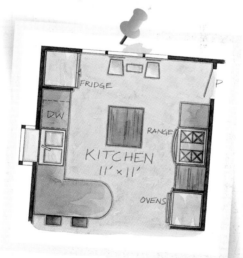

two-triangle kitchen In this layout, an island adds prep space and helps direct traffic in a space with two workstations. Two cooks need not cross each other's paths while they work. The resulting two triangles can share a leg, often anchored at the refrigerator.

Customize stock items for affordable style. Make a standard wooden countertop fit an island by purchasing a second section; cut it to size and glue it to both ends of the top. Standard end pieces finish it off.

beyond the WOODS

This kitchen once had oak cupboards, oak floors, and oak trees just outside the windows. Then, the 30-year-old scheme stepped into the light.

There are some skeptics who can't imagine painting oak cabinets. But homeowner Jean Norman knew "guts"-ing up and grabbing the paint was key to brightening the kitchen. This former editor of *Do It Yourself* magazine admits, in a cobbler's children-type tale, that over the years she had let the space go stale, dated, and dark. So she and her husband, Ben, put their expert DIY skills to work, in what they they think of as their best collaboration to date.

Besides brightening the oak cabinets with white paint, the Normans freshened their oak island with a soft blue to turn it into a focal point. White solid-surfacing countertops polish off the lighter look and cue the soft gray wall color. The other big changes involved bumping back one wall to add space and storage and camouflaging popcorn-textured ceilings with affordable, 4×8-foot sheets of exterior paneling. New X-shape mullions in the upper cabinets and on the island strike a sophisticated note, backed up by mercury glass pendants, updated pulls and knobs, and floor-to-ceiling curtains. Crisp patterns on fabrics, wallpaper, and rugs add another layer of color, further lifting the kitchen's spirit.

Even small details play along in the lively update. Ball fringe, fun accessories, and a chandelier strung with beads bring fun and fresh style to the kitchen. The best part? Many of the Normans' ideas can be accomplished even if you don't have their expert-level DIY talents.

opposite: Jean and Ben updated every surface in their '80s kitchen, except the original oak floors. They added select new features, such as an undermount sink and a counter-depth fridge.

Budget Breakdown:

Sink & faucet	$500
Counters	$2,200
Refrigerator	$800
Cooktop	$400
Ceiling paneling	$300
Chandeliers	$100
Pendant lights	$420
Hardware	$250
Total:	**$4,970**

the problem

A new stainless-steel refrigerator only made the rest of this kitchen more dowdy by comparison. **the solution:** Though the owners didn't want to invest big dollars in a remodeling, clever DIY ideas created worthy surroundings for the chic appliance.

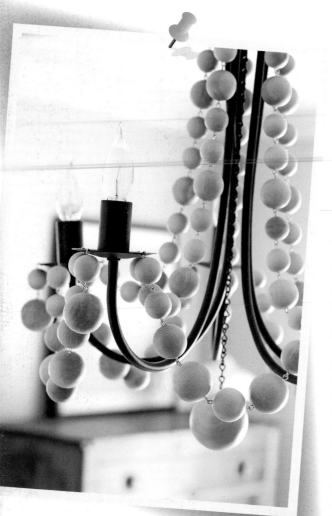

pricey looks for less

Ideas for getting custom style at off-the-rack prices.

Be inspired by the best. Design-savvy Jean spotted chic wooden chandeliers in an upscale boutique. But $2,500 was a wee bit out of her price range. So she and Ben came up with an affordable and unique solution *(left)*: Ben strung together wooden beads with eye hooks and swagged them over discount-store fixtures.

Mix old and new. The contrast of old and new, woodsy and slick, makes a space more interesting. In the adjoining dining room, clean, crisply patterned fabrics, along with low-cost but high-design side chairs, put the mod on a country table and classic Hitchcock chairs.

Custom looks for less cash. Funky, oversize ball fringe transforms ready-made matchstick blinds from the home improvement store into designer coverings.

Instant art. Jean gets creative and crafty to decorate her walls. Hanging from standard office-supply jumbo clips, two favorite plates become eye-grabbing art pieces.

diy tip

Plumbing pipes have a steely coo. That, and the fact that you can have them cut to measure at a hardware store, make them excellent curtain rods. Shop for giant grommets at fabric stores or sites (they come with a tool to install them), and all you need to do is hem the fabric.

Moving a wall back 24 inches made room for a new base cabinet that's a perfect serving station. On the back door, two shades of paint add the illusion of raised panels (use painter's tape to mark off your designs).

Cutting and fitting basic lumber is easier than working with curvy crown molding and creates a clean country look. Standard materials—4×8-foot siding panels and 1×2, 1×3, and 1×4 pine boards—give the ceiling a custom look on a modest budget.

Anchor an island by painting it a darker shade than the rest of your cabinets and by adding a countertop made of a contrasting material, such as wood.

10 DIY Ideas to Steal

PUT YOUR OWN DATED KITCHEN ON THE PATH TO RECOVERY BY ADOPTING THESE DOABLE FACELIFT IDEAS.

1. Repeat Xs and Os

Give continuity to a design by repeating elements. Here, Xs on cabinet doors, island end caps, and host chairs team up for impact. The same is true for the Os that appear on the knobs, rug, shade and chandelier trim, and melamine plates used as cheap wall art. Now that's design rhythm.

2

Select a better sink

A 30-inch base cabinet meant a too-small sink for the original kitchen. Now, a new undermount, single-bowl sink made especially for a 30-inch cabinet features inside measurements of 28×16 inches. At 10 inches deep, it hides dirty dishes with ease. Plus, it's easy to wipe food waste directly from the counter into the sink. The bonus of an undercounter sink: no nasty caulk to clean.

3. Paint your cabinets

The process starts with paint prep and a high-quality primer. These doors and drawer fronts were spray-painted, but you can get a smooth finish with self-leveling paint and a mohair roller. If the finish still isn't smooth enough, roll on the paint, then use a paintbrush to quickly brush it in one direction.

4

Invest in knobs and pulls

Hardware can completely change the look of cabinets. Make sure existing hinges match the style and finish of the new hardware unless European hinges can be used.

5. Curtain it off

Visually mark the dividing line between kitchen and dining rooms with curtains hung from the ceiling. Open, they create the feeling of two spaces. Closed, they hide the kitchen's work area from Thanksgiving dinner.

6. Cover the plugs

The best idea you can't see? Replacing electrical outlets in the backsplash with a power strip that's attached to the bottom of the upper cabinets. More outlets; no clutter.

7

Splurge on something you love

Savings count when redoing a kitchen, but leave room in the budget to splurge as well. The marble-look solid-surfacing counters elevate this redo. They're durable, classic, and will look great for years.

8. Hang art one roll at a time

A single roll of wallpaper makes a big design splash. Use it on an accent wall rather than throughout the kitchen.

9

Light with flair

These mercury glass pendants offer sophistication, durability, and task lighting. In most kitchens the island lighting should be the most dramatic in the room. It also needs to provide plenty of light for working.

10. Try butcher block

This affordable option from a discount store costs only $195 for a piece about 73×40 inches. Protect the counter with several light coats of a food-safe salad-bowl finish.

diy tip

Ditch the single overhead light fixture in favor of pendants, track lighting, and task lamps. Use a mirror to bounce light into dark places.

it's all about
THE BLUE

This tiny galley kitchen was once as welcoming as a black hole. Then out went the dark colors and dim lighting, and in came the sparkle and color.

When Lacey Howard first laid eyes on this cottage, she fell in love with every room—except one. The kitchen was small, dark, and uninspiring. Luckily, Lacey has some visionary skills. This decorating editor and style expert saw past the heavy '80s color scheme and bad lighting to the sparkling gem it could be. To plan for its transformation and keep it on budget, Lacey started a file of inspirational photos, paint chips, and fabric swatches. "The key to budget remodeling is to think before you gut the space," Lacey says.

Tops on Lacey's wish list: a fresh palette, a pretty seat for the existing bay window, and better lighting. "As I was clipping photos from magazines," she says, "I noticed I was drawn to blue kitchens." The cool blue color she picked perked the room right up, especially when set off by crisp black and white. She could live with the existing neutral floor and countertop, so they stayed, freeing funds for more dramatic changes, such as a sparkly tile backsplash and an expanded entryway.

Like many galley kitchens, Lacey's suffered from a lack of light. Neither budget nor space allowed for new windows, so she opened up the wall between her kitchen and dining room. This visually opened up the space and scooped in more light, giving the kitchen an airy, open feeling. To keep the good feeling going, Lacey removed bulky upper cabinets above the stove and replaced them with reflective glass shelves. Bright dishware stays out and at the ready for more fun and function.

opposite: With help from a creative contractor, Lacey made big changes in her home's tiny kitchen. For about $4,500, she has a modern space suitable for cocktail parties or morning coffee.

✓ **Budget Breakdown:**

Paint	$144
Lighting	$197
Cabinet pulls	$120
Fabric	$120
Trash can	$27
Glass shelves	$102
Tile	$185
Labor	$3,620
Total:	**$4,515**

before

Classic but affordable white subway tile looks fresh when installed on a dynamic angle.

the problem
Bland walls and cranberry cabinets shouted "outdated '80s style." The small galley space also lacked windows and light. New windows weren't in the budget.
the solution: A fresh color palette and reflective surfaces brought bright vibes to this kitchen.

THE PALETTE:
bold but pretty

Are you ready to go for a brighter palette? You are if you:
_Take color cues from the pages of fave fashion mags.
_Have Design*Sponge in your RSS feed.
_Throw parties with gal pals when the IKEA catalog hits your mailbox.
_Love color, and aren't afraid to wear it or live with it.

WALL
This happy shade radiates confidence.

Candid Blue,
Sherwin-Williams

TRIM
Crisp white brightens up small spaces.

Snowbound,
Sherwin-Williams

CABINETS
Gray is hot, hot, hot on the home decor runway.

Iron Ore,
Sherwin-Williams

ACCENT
Buttery yellow pops against blue hues.

Midday,
Sherwin-Williams

Your local hardware or home improvement store will cut glass shelves to size. Install them on sleek and simple brackets and the barely-there shelves allow collections to pop.

diy tip

For sewing projects, think outside the bolt. Expand a fabric search to linens and designer remnants. Lacey snagged fabrics from tag sales and discount shops long before the redo, sticking to a black-and-white palette for easy mixing. Black trim outlines and separates the motifs.

how to:
find the right contractor

Lacey is first to admit her kitchen redo was a team effort. Though flush with design ideas, this style editor knew her DIY skills weren't a match her good eye. So she set about finding the right partners for the project. Seeking referrals from friends and researching on her own, Lacey found Rochelle Travato and her business partner, Jeff Timmerman. One conversation and she knew they were different from the other contractors. Here's her advice on finding an expert you gel with.

Get a reality check. Here are some questions to get the conversation going: How long have you been in the business? Are you licensed or registered with the state? (This is important for large projects or if plumbing and electrical work is involved.) How many projects like mine have you done? Do you have images of those and a list of references?

Make sure you're on the same page. Your partners should be as enthusiastic about the project as you are. "When I whipped out my wish list," says Lacey, "Ro's eyes lit up. I knew then we spoke the same language." Not only did they trust her design instincts, they reassured her there were ways to make budget by reusing and recycling—an important aspect of the project for Lacey. "I get jobs because I actually listen to my clients," says Travato. "I love design, so that makes it easy to get excited about what they want and love."

Get reassurance. Contract requirements vary by state. Even if your state doesn't require a written agreement, you should ask for one. A contract spells out the who, what, where, and how much of your project.

stage 1 Sometimes, making design decisions on the fly is the best way to go. You get a chance to see the changes in progress and react. Once the upper cabinets were painted white and glass mosaic tile was in place, Lacey decided to paint the lower cabinets charcoal, sensing more white would be too much.

stage 2 The blue, black, gray, and white glass tile visually bridges the white upper cabinets with the dark lower ones. The team decided to update the window seat with doors for extra storage. They painted it charcoal to underscore the window's architecture.

stage 3 When the blue paint was finished, Lacey paused for a few days. She wondered if it was too much for the small space. It didn't take her long to decide the shade was just right. Once she layered on crisp and sophisticated black and white prints, the room became color-balanced. The fabrics also countered the hard surfaces with a soft touch.

$5,000 Budget

diy tip

If green is your goal, shop unexpected places. Check salvage shops and the local Habitat for Humanity Restores bargains. Or call contractors and flooring shops to ask about remnants.

style with a
PURPOSE

A tiny lake cottage offered this family a chance to show its decorating bravado and DIY know-how. It all starts with a sunshine palette.

Katy Gannon-Janelle steered her—and her family's—considerable do-it-yourself drive into their lake home's fresh, fun redo. The small, seasonal cottage allowed her to relax her usually traditional style and perk up her palette, especially in the kitchen—the darkest spot in the place. "The color palette was the starting point," says Katy, "which was partly in reaction to what the house was like when we bought it—dark brown and gray. I wanted to counteract the darkness with some eternal sunshine."

Rich yellows, pale woods, and smooth white banished the darkness in the open kitchen and dining area. Dark wood counters ground the surfaces and add definition to the space. They're joined by a vintage trestle table, one of many pieces Katy and her husband, Pierre, culled from her basement and attic. Some get a dose of fun paint color; all are part of a bigger picture of recycled style in this home. "We wanted to use a lot of recycled and natural products that would feel appropriate in a vacation home in a lakeside setting," she says.

Eco-chic bamboo floors underscore her point. The narrow, but sturdy, planks are easy-care—another bonus. And the family painted on the happy color with low-VOC paints. "This house is only 8 to 10 feet from the water," she says, "and we didn't want to do anything to harm the lake."

Simple built-ins and benches create seating in a slip of space and give daughter Charlotte a canvas for her original artwork. Just one more brilliant stroke in this labor of love.

opposite: The Janelle family got busy with the crowbars and hammers, removing heavy cabinetry in favor of a slender island and a pantry cupboard built by local craftsmen.

✓ **Budget Breakdown:**

Counters	$700
Cabinets	$2,000
Appliances	$1,200
Floor	$500
Beaded board	$75
Faucet	$295
Paint	$150
Industrial lights	$100
Total:	**$5,020**

Highlight a breakfast nook by painting its walls a different color from the walls and ceilings of the surrounding area

before

the problem
The kitchen was the darkest room in this sunny lake house. **the solution:** Let the sunshine in with yellow paint and reflective surfaces.

10 DIY Ideas to Steal

KEEP THE HEART OF YOUR HOME HEALTHY WITH PRODUCTS THAT ARE ALL ABOUT GOING GREEN AND SAVING GREEN. HERE ARE 10 EASY, INEXPENSIVE WAYS TO RE-CREATE THIS CLEAN-LINED KITCHEN.

1. Sleek and chic
Invest in a pull-down faucet that's both fabulous and functional. Some come with awesome extras, like a water-saving pause function.

2. Go bamboo
Installing this renewable resource for your flooring makes you feel good about what's under your feet.

3. Paint without pause
There are many types of low-VOC paints on the market—some even made with chocolate and fiber! All are a healthier alternative to most paints for both you and the environment.

4. Bright backsplash
Beaded board can soften sharp lines in a modern kitchen. A bright color breaking through a coat of roughed-up white paint adds a pop of personality. Try easy-to-install paneled sheets.

5. Caged in
Create a hardworking kitchen with affordable industrial-style lighting.

6. Save your energy
Purchase appliances, electronics, and even lighting with the Energy Star stamp of approval. They use 20–30 percent less energy than required by federal standards and pay for themselves in energy savings.

7. Stunning simplicity
The streamlined style of flat cabinets gives the kitchen a modern feel. Add sleek hardware and they look great—without overpowering a space.

8. Pushing paper
Shop for counters made from 100 percent post-consumer recycled office paper or cardboard. And they're affordable, too.

9. Unfinished business
This stool is a blank canvas, so do with it what you please. Line three or four up along a kitchen island, and paint to your liking.

10. Faking it
Copy Katy and get the cool-as-steel look for your stools with metallic paints.

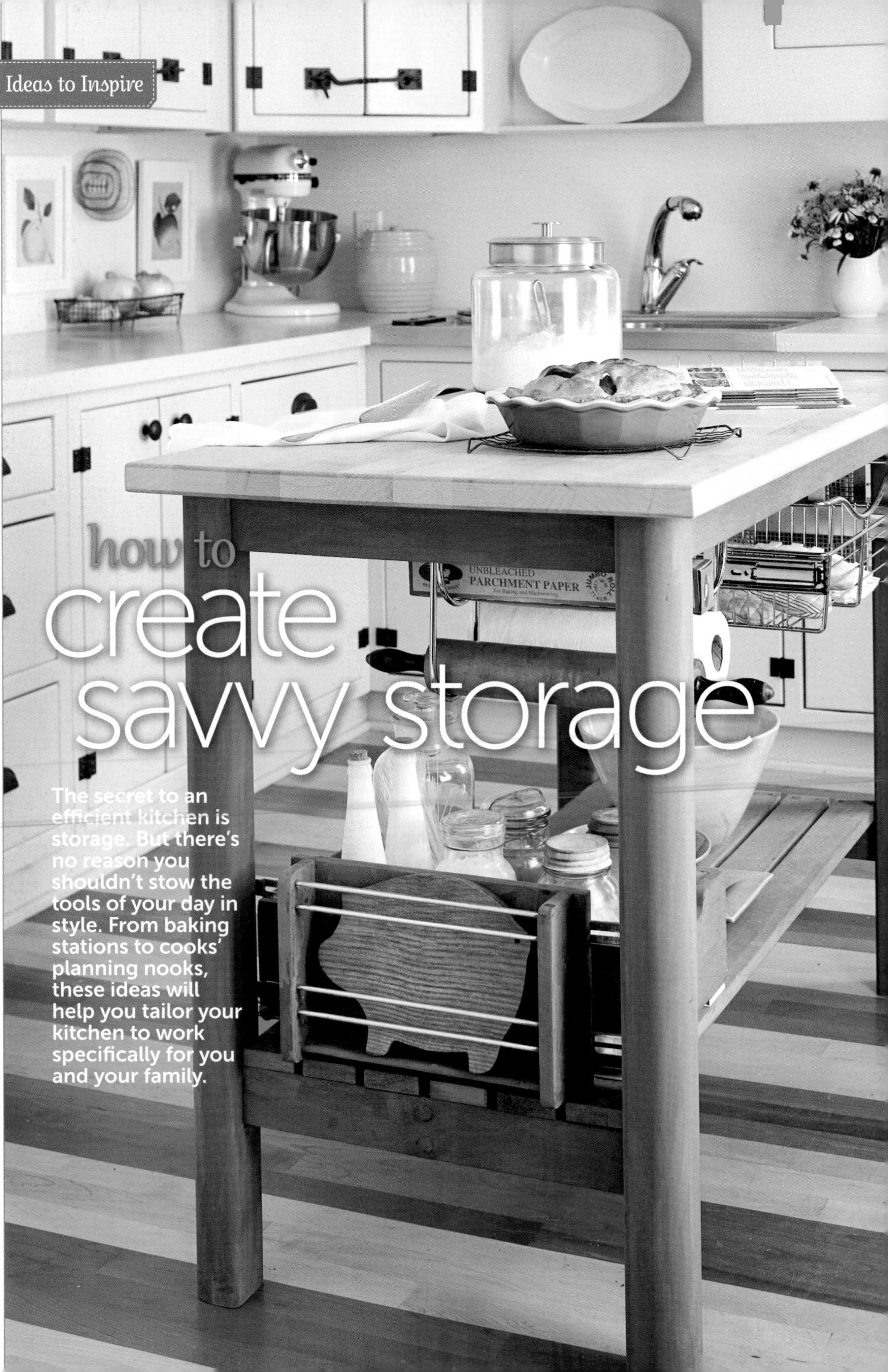
UNBLEACHED
PARCHMENT PAPER
For Baking and Microwaving
JUMBO ROLL

how to create savvy storage

The secret to an efficient kitchen is storage. But there's no reason you shouldn't stow the tools of your day in style. From baking stations to cooks' planning nooks, these ideas will help you tailor your kitchen to work specifically for you and your family.

savvy storage
rack and roll

Customize an island for how you cook.

To maximize your kitchen without remodeling, modify *an unfinished island* with clever add-ons found in any home center. This one, *opposite,* corrals supplies for a homemaker who likes to bake. *Drawers, racks, and hooks* hold ingredients and tools for a full-service station. The island was bought off the shelf and assembled with *a screwdriver and power drill.* The 4×2-foot work surface is spacious enough for rolling out pastry.

1. See-through stash. An undermount wire drawer keeps items in plain view. Attach 1×3-inch wood strips to the underside of the island top and mount racks to the strips.
2. Handy hang-ups. Keep frequently used spices at your fingertips on a two-tier hanging rack suspended from a matching bar. Slip on a hanging utensil holder as well.
3. Repurposed pieces. Turns out, wine racks are ideal for holding baking supplies. Install a rack on the island's underside. Below it, a pullout drawer glides from a lower shelf that was created from 1×3 boards.
4. Edgy style. A cutting board holder comes with metal side rails that attach to the island's legs.

savvy storage
box office

Make your work spot more productive.

A slice of counter or small desk will be
better prepared to tackle household mail
and papers if you top it with an open wall
cabinet, *above,* that has an adjustable
shelf to fit boxes and binders for receipts
and records. Below the boxed storage,
corkboard panels create a memo board.
The framed panels are ready to hang.

savvy storage
tech center

Wire a world of electronics into one little space.

A doorless cabinet, *opposite,* holds a television,
recharging station, and wireless printer. For
a techy office bulletin board, lean magnetic
boards against the wall. (These hide cords as a
bonus.) Fasten important papers to the boards
with magnets and keep supplies in sight with
transparent office containers that stack on
overhead shelves.

Personalize the space with supersize initials created on a sleek little portable printer and framed for fun.

savvy storage
cook's nook

Every cook deserves a cool menu-planning spot.

This personal work spot, *opposite,* brings recipes, meal plans, and grocery lists together. Remove the doors of existing cabinets or buy stock cabinets for cookbooks. Create a recipe stash with a rod and spice baskets. Standing in as a clever memo board, muffin tins have magnetic qualities.

savvy storage
kids' stop

Create a kid-friendly corner for fun and function.

Connect school and home with familiar supplies and chalkboard elements. Brushed with chalkboard paint, the doors of a 15-inch bridge cabinet, *above,* hide necessities and school papers too good to toss. Below, inexpensive school calendars slip in and out of simple ready-made frames.

1

2

3

4

rethink cabinets

Turn odds-and-ends stock cabinetry into stylish stashes.

A mishmash of *stock cabinets, cubbies, and doors* offers the framework for a storage wall and island, *opposite*. A couple of coats of *energetic paint* erase any differences in the cabinets' style and details. Select components to match your storage needs. A cobbled-together island started life as *drawers and matching narrow cupboards*. The storage pieces are encased in *two hollow-core doors* cut to fit and laminated.

1. Swing time. Avoid the busy look of too much open shelving by concealing the lower part of the cabinet with a panel of fabric suspended from a swing-arm rod.
2. Hang tough. Keep countertops clean and clutter-free by suspending screw-top glass canisters from a purchased handle and a section of heavy-gauge wire.
3. Customize cupboards. With shelves that are adjusted to fit and labeled, the skinny cupboards in the island can keep a sizable cookbook collection close at hand.
4. Stow and go. Niches—open or hidden behind a flap of fabric—make handy appliance garages.

A mix of new and salvaged materials give this island one-of-a-kind character. Galvanized steel drawers slide out to reveal a linen stash.

linens

makeovers on a
$10,000 budget

128   134   140   146   154   160   166

diy tip

For a clean and airy look, keep patterns to a minimum. Composite counters and mellow wood grains add texture and interest, but showstopping pattern is reserved for the tile floor.

country
CLEANS UP

This kitchen is a little bit country and a little bit rock 'n' roll, thanks to mellow materials and clean, retro lines.

For Christi Jensen, creating a stylish kitchen on the cheap was the goal. But this devotee of handcrafted goods and do-it-yourself diva also wanted to marry modern looks and function with the rest of the house—a nostalgic bungalow—with an up-to-date Arts and-Crafts vibe. Sounds like big plans for someone with only a small chunk of change to play with, unless you follow Christi's basic tenet: "Don't be afraid!" she says. "Even with a small budget there are things you can do to make your kitchen work better and look cuter."

Christi turned DIY gutsiness into design success by hitting books, magazines, and her laptop, for both inspiration and action. "Do your research," she says, "lots and lots of research. I would suggest using online tools. IKEA offers a great planner that really helped us get started."

Using flat-pack, off-the-shelf cabinetry, Christi replaced worn-out cupboards and shaky, open shelves with streamlined cabinets in a mix of standard and ultra tall, slim configurations. She fit them with inserts to help her keep her young family and new business running smoothly. She also swapped outdated appliances with professional-looking, stainless-steel ones she found at a discount home store.

Christi created her clean, classic style by designing to both sides of the equation: mellow woods and beaded-board paneling balance stainless steel and creamy composite counters. Without using a heavy hand with color, pattern, or accessories, she created a look that's open, airy, and always organized.

opposite: Lightly dressed or uncovered window architecture joins with simple design elements for a look that is open and uplifting. Medium wood tones and a touch of texture keep it grounded.

✓ **Budget Breakdown:**

Wall paint	$75
Cabinetry	$4,000
Sink	$313
Appliances	$3,800
Faucet	$179
Flooring	$500
Misc.	$150
Total:	**$9,017**

the problem

The cramped and outdated galley kitchen lacked useful storage necessary to stash supplies for entertaiing family and friends. **the solution:** Bring down too-high cabinets and remake a new lower bank with inserts that keep things tidy.

Mix textures and styles for a more interesting personality. Stainless-steel shelves look clean and cool juxtaposed with a beaded board backsplash.

the right details

Pay attention to the little things in a kitchen remodel to get a custom look for less cash.

Sweeten with stainless. Purchase sleek stainless-steel appliances from home improvement stores or other discount outlets. You'll get the look for less if you don't need pro power but want a chef's style.

Get custom look-alikes. Opting out of upper cabinets and leaving the exhaust hood exposed opens the space and creates a gourmet look in this kitchen. A small, add-on shelf keeps olive oil, spices, and potted herbs within easy reach while the cook is whipping up dinner.

Find the perfect fit. The tidy bank of cabinets on the long wall of this galley kitchen means more storage for kitchen necessities. But that wasn't enough for this homeowner, who took it one step further by installing drawer inserts for extra organization.

diy tip

By moving the range to the same wall as the refrigerator, Christi created a more efficient layout. Having the sink centered between expanses of countertop lends the space a more open feeling.

diy tip

Creating a built-in desk in your kitchen is easy using countertops and cabinets. Select a lightweight counter material that can span enough space to tuck legs under without needing support underneath.

how to install:
laminate tile flooring

Materials:

_Tile
_Straight-back handsaw
_Keyhole saw or jigsaw
_Fitting wedges
_Pry bar

DIY tips

Use an underlayment foam with a vapor barrier on concrete subfloors.

In damp (or potentially damp) areas, seal all expansion spaces with **mildew-resistant silicone.**

step 1

Saw off the tongue on the upper and left sides of the first tile. Begin laying tiles in the left-hand corner of the room. Use wedges to maintain a $\frac{3}{8}$-inch gap from the wall. For all first-row tiles, saw off the tongue on the wall-facing side. Always saw tiles with the finshed surface facing up.

step 2

Click the next tile in place, lifting it slightly and then pressing down to lock. Continue clicking tiles in place along the room's width. Cut the last panel in the row to length.

step 3

Install the next row by clicking together tiles to form a panel that runs the width of the room. Click the entire panel into place with the first row. Install additional rows using the same technique. To fit the final row, cut tiles to size and join together with a pry bar. Finish with base or quarter-round molding and T-strips at the doorways.

What she did...

To put snappier style underfoot, Christi got creative with inexpensive, do-it-yourself laminate squares. The 12x12 squares can be easy to overlook unless you do what Christi did and install them in an unexpected, focal-point pattern.

diy tip

Extending their budget by painting their 1990s hickory cabinets and sticking closely to the original footprint allowed the Egen family to pop for new appliances. "We did things economically without compromising on quality," Alma says.

an *instant* CLASSIC

This kitchen went from builder bland to custom elegant—a better fit for the 19th-century home—thanks to one couple's DIY know-how.

Nothing could stop the Egens from redoing their kitchen—not budget or two small kids, not even snakes. These dedicated do-it-yourselfers have encountered the unexpected while working on remodeling projects, but even they were surprised by the unwelcome guests that appeared when they renovated the kitchen in their 1861 Greek Revival house. Bradley and Alma Moore-Egen found a hole in the floor under one base cabinet, and then they found a nest of Eastern milk snakes. "We always wondered why our cats were so interested in the old base cabinets," says Alma.

Once the wildlife was evicted, the creative couple spent 11 months making their dream kitchen a reality. Working weekends as time and money allowed, they enlisted the help of friends and relatives, recycling and transforming what they could in the 22×17-foot space. "The old kitchen had a tight layout with little counter space," Alma says. "All the counter space, cabinets, and appliances were crammed into one corner, and the rest of the room was empty."

Bradley and Alma kept the sink where it was to save costs but replaced and rejiggered the other appliances. "Keeping things close to their original location helped us keep costs down," says Alma. The two also sanded and painted the existing cabinets. The upper cabinets were topped with a 12-inch board-and-crown molding to give them height. Bargain shopping filled the gaps. "Working on our house is our favorite hobby," says Alma. "We loved every minute of it."

opposite: Alma stole moments for hands-on projects in her kitchen. She grouted the backsplash tile one afternoon while the kids napped. "It turned out much easier than I expected," she says.

✓ Budget Breakdown:

Dishwasher	$1,200
Range & accessories	$1,750
Refrigerator	$2,350
Sink	$1,250
Cabinets	$200
Island	$200
Counters	$1,100
Tile	$150
Cabinet paint & trim	$900
Total:	**$9,100**

A range hood with a shallow shelf and plate rack was constructed from stock lumber.

The homeowners made this island from an antique tailor's table they'd had for years. A wood base brings it to counter height; the stainless-steel top adds a sleek, cleanable touch.

The couple's favorite splurge is the custom fabricated sink. Because they kept their stock cabinets, they had to have one made to fit...so why not make it a cool one?

the problem

Hickory cabinets and floor created a dull sameness, and the overall style was devoid of personality.
the solution: This couple went to work, aging the cupboards with paint and upping their style quotient with crown molding and custom touches.

BREAD

Alma found wood knobs on closeout sale for a buck each, and painted them along with the rest of the cabinets. Painting lower cabinets black anchors the room and adds vintage elegance.

sanity-saving tips

Thinking of tackling a kitchen remodel? The Egens have some advice for surviving what can be a topsy-turvy process for your family:

Plan ahead. Order your materials and have everything sorted and on hand before you do any work.

Hold onto the big picture. Post an inspirational shot from a book, magazine, or website to remind you of what you're working toward.

Make yourself at home. Set up a makeshift kitchen somewhere in the house so you don't have to go out for every meal.

Look for bartered labor. Enlist the help of friends and family. How to get them on board? Simple. "Beer and pizza," says Alma.

Take your sweet time. Spread the rehab project over a realistic time period. Factor in enough time you know you can dedicate to working on your project.

diy tip

Polished wood is one of the most cost-efficient counter surfaces. These cherry, butcher-block countertops are easy for a DIYer with moderate skills to install; they will last a long time with a heavy-duty seal.

BREAD

4 ways to add more drama

No one likes a lot of drama—but a little bit of bold adds personality and punch to a kitchen area. Steal these ideas for your project:

1. SPLURGE WHERE IT COUNTS. Farmhouse sinks have the size and look to be a real focal point. But reproduction or salvaged models can be tough to retrofit into cabinets of a certain age. Contact a local kitchen design shop for someone who can fabricate a looker like this one, crafted of galvanized metal.

2. RECYCLE AND RETHINK EXISTING PIECES. Antique chairs have their own personality, and their classic curves can add sculptural interest to a kitchen or breakfast nook. A not-so-old table plays along when given the same aged paint treatment as the lower cabinets. Modern art and a simple iron chandelier freshen the style with their simple lines.

3. TURN ON RESTAURANT STYLE. Not too tough on the checkbook, this stainless-steel backsplash, pot-filler faucet, and spice shelf add style with substance, especially when framed by a wood range hood that is pieced together from off-the-shelf trim and stock lumber.

4. CREATE BEAUTY WITH BUILT-INS. Have a partial wall or niche in your kitchen that isn't working as hard as it should? This empty wall was treated to new cabinetry that surrounds the refrigerator, hides the microwave, and provides more pantry storage and display shelving.

diy tip

In the absence of upper cabinets, take time to determine what gear is essential. Put these items on open shelves, hang them from bars, or slip them on hooks. Stash other items in lower cabinets or a pantry.

break out
OF THE BOX

This compact 9×10 kitchen was top-heavy and square—not a good look. But it did have its good features, which one DIY expert played up with cosmetics.

Dark cabinets and paneling, low ceilings, and a tight space can really cramp a kitchen's style. The good news is, lightening up isn't all that hard to do. In this boxy little kitchen, designer Wade Scherrer started with a crowbar, taking down upper cabinets and paring down an oversize header that housed flourescent lighting (the flourescents and their cool, green light went, too). With those heavy features out of the way, the kitchen's light-emitting bank of windows become a clear focal point. Covering the rest of the surfaces—including the downer brown paneling—with creamy semigloss paint, countertops, and tile gives the room a lift and makes it appear larger.

Other fool-the-eye tricks keep the new brightened attitude going. Simple matchstick blinds are cut to span three windows, limiting the number of cords and visual breaks for a cleaner look. Stainless-steel appliances, while a splurge, add enough contrast and gleam to stand off against the white cupboards.

In this small house, remaking the kitchen's looks wasn't enough; Scherrer needed to make it work more efficiently as well. With the removal of the top cupboards, clever, ultra-organized storage was top on the list. New stock and custom-fit inserts turned the lower cupboards into more efficient—and more easily accessible—storage. Upgrading a few pieces of cookware in pretty colors means they double as accessories, doing their best to play up both the fun and functional side of the kitchen's character.

opposite: Redoing the bulkhead raised that part of the ceiling by six inches and made the room feel bigger. Keeping the backgrounds the same creamy color further opens up the space.

✓ Budget Breakdown:	
Cabinetry	$3,200
Range	$1,500
Refrigerator	$1,200
Dishwasher	$600
Tile	$750
Counters	$1,500
Blinds	$500
Sink & faucet	$400
Total:	**$9,650**

diy tip

Paint window frames to match the surrounding walls to blend the two elements and minimize visual clutter. Take tile to the ceiling for a durable and cleanable surface that only looks expensive.

before

he problem

high-contrast color palette and full cupboards
hop up this small U-shape family kitchen.
he solution: A clean, neutral scheme of wheat
nd white opens up the space. Baskets and clever
etrofitted cubbies and inserts add efficient
torage with less heavy cabinetry.

beguiling tiling

The designer dressed up the walls in this kitchen with
stonelike tiles, giving the space subtle texture, pattern, and
personality. Here are some of his favorite tips for stylish tile.

Criss-cross for class. Install wall
tile in a diagonal patern to disguise
the fact that windows aren't quite
level and walls are cattywampus.
Plus, diagonal designs fool your
eye into seeing a larger space.
Get creative with crevices. Tile
on a wall receives much less wear
than on a floor, so explore grout
colors. You can confidently choose
grout a shade lighter or brighter
than your tile. Keep it close to
the shade of tile you choose,
however, or you will create a busy
pattern of lines.
Net some easy beauty. For easy-
to-install tile accents, choose
premade borders and mosaics that
are sold glued to mesh material
that can quickly be cut to size.

how to:
install pullout shelves

Line cabinet trays with rubber-coated shelf paper or another nonslip surfacing to keep plates in their place and glassware upright.

The only tools you need to have on hand are:

_Measuring tape

_Extra nuts and bolts

_Power drill

DIY tips

Count all the pieces. Before you start installing the inserts, check off all the pieces and parts to make sure an essential piece isn't missing before you build.

Cover up. Thoroughly clean the cupboards before installing inserts, and make certain to cover rough or worn surfaces with scrubbable or cleanable shelf paper.

Easy liftoff. Baskets and sliding trays should be easily removed for their cleaning, and so you can keep the entire cupboard clean.

How to install cupboard inserts.

Installing new base cabinets with rolling trays offers ready access to your dinnerware or pots and pans. If you're retrofitting inserts, however, it's easier to install wire types. You can also make existing drawers more organized by making wood dividers from extra lumber or moldings. Or shop for ready-made drawer trays that have partitions to keep small bits and pieces in their place.

step 1
Assemble before you insert.
Connect multiple elements using the hardware provided with the insert kit. Test-fit the units in the cabinet box, trimming to size where necessary.

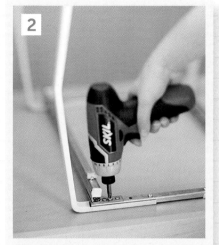

step 2
Mark and predrill holes.
Use a bit that is an appropriate size for the mounting screws. Drive in drywall or wood screws with a power drill to avoid using hand tools in the tight, awkward space.

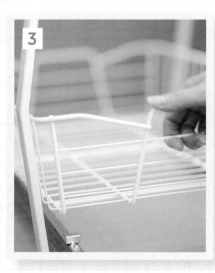

step 3
Attach and let it slide.
Install baskets, bins, and other storage accessories. Lubricate any rails or moving parts with spray silicone to assure a smooth ride.

step 4
Make use of every inch.
Store tall and flat items—such as baking sheets, platters, and serving trays—in the gaps along the sides of the insert.

Shop for organizational pieces that go vertical so you can stow layers of items without gobbling too much counter space.

so chic, SO SIMPLE

This kitchen is elegant enough for entertaining and efficient enough for serious cooking. Best of all, it's as cost-conscious as it is cool.

Creamy beige is like a chef's pure white plate, says homeowner Karin Edwards. "Both are a perfect backdrop for whatever you want to show off," she says. "In my case, that's my food and my friends." And she wanted that backdrop to be high-style and low-fuss.

But high style often comes with a high price. Sleek lines mean flush-set appliances, custom-designed cabinetry, and hidden outlets, among other things. And Karin's budget hovered around $10,000. It was time to get creative with her dated '70s kitchen, with its torn linoleum and faux-oak cabinets.

Fortunately the house, a 1950s flat-roof, offered motivation. "It's sited on a hilltop, with windows on three sides to look out on a sprawling lawn of century-old oaks," she says. "The views are so stunning, they make you take on the craziest projects."

The only thing to do was simplify. Karin chopped the square room into three parts: a tidy galley with only as much prep space as she needed, a walk-in pantry for extra storage, and a laundry closet for a washer and dryer that used to sit by the kitchen sink. The galley was an economical decision. Karin sliced her cabinet costs by one-third. The walk-in pantry holds the excess, as do two tall pullout units that flank the fridge.

Style tricks saved more money and upped the chic quotient. Instead of tile, Karin installed a croc-texture wallcovering of washable vinyl, glued to a board and framed in chrome. "I learned along the way that the only way to get the work done," she says, "is to just relax and have fun with it."

opposite: A stainless-steel drop-in sink with built-in drainboard and laminate counters are home improvement store bargains. Faux-crocodile wallcovering is a clever stand-in for expensive tile.

✓ Budget Breakdown:

Dishwasher	$500
Cooktop & oven	$4,130
Range hood	$370
Countertop	$300
Sink	$130
Faucet	$100
Cabinetry	$3,220
Lighting	$345
Total:	**$9,095**

For a more interesting, cove-look ceiling, Karin painted a wide band around the perimeter darker than the walls. The banding idea repeats on a tailored Roman shade for a designer touch.

Bring accessories into the kitchen that are normally found elsewhere for a style surprise.

When her off-the-shelf cabinets didn't fit precisely, Karin made an open cubby for spices and lined its interior with leftover tile.

Ceramic tile is affordable flooring that is available in hundreds of colors and looks. For a modern flavor, select large, 16×16-inch squares.

before

the problem

This dowdy kitchen was last remodeled in the 1970s with inexpensive materials that were falling apart.
the solution: Shrink the square space into a galley, adding a wall to create a large walk-in pantry. That saves enough in cabinet costs to splurge on high-end appliances.

character at cost

Tips on where—and how—to save decorating dollars.

Make fake built-ins. Tall storage units surround the refrigerator to give it a bulit-in look for less.

Be open to all materials. Though she dreamed of real stone counters, Karin compromised when she found reversible laminate counters that pop in and out of their frame. The creamy shade was just right for her scheme.

Find look-alikes for fancy surfaces. Washable, vinyl wallcovering is a sturdy, money-saving alternative to tile. In a crocodile pattern, it looks way chic. Mosaic glass tile was used only above the range. Ceramic floor tile is great at mimicking pricier natural stone. Select ceramics in natural colors such as this sueded concrete look.

Be ready to downsize. Karin's square kitchen had too much dead space in the middle of the floor. So she divided it into zones that include a walk-in pantry, a laundry closet, and a smaller galley kitchen.

diy tip

By adding a wall along
one side of a kitchen,
you can create laundry
and pantry space that's
easy to access. Easy-
hang, utilitarian shelves
are much less expensive
than cabinets.

6 ways to add affordable chic

When you're short on cash but want a Champagne-elegant look, it's time to get creative.

1. LIGHTING. Stainless-steel shelves were mounted upside down and drilled to hold puck lights. Outlets hide along the back edge of the shelf.

2. DISPLAY. Carving out a niche in a doorway made room for wine cubbies and glass display shelves for cookbooks and stemware.

3. STORAGE. You can never have enough of it, especially in a small kitchen. Wire pullouts like these (found at most home centers) make the most of any storage space—and put things in easy reach.

4. FAKES. Washable faux-crocodile vinyl wallcovering takes the place of pricier tile. The tile is installed only where needed, such as behind the cooktop.

5. CABINETS. All the sleek white and beige cabinetry was purchased flat-pack and installed by a carpenter. Small, flip-up cupboards take the place of large upper cabinets and are easily accessed.

6. SAVE AND SPLURGE. This cook saved so much on cabinetry, she could splurge for what she really wanted in appliances. Professionally styled and powered appliances sit flush with the cabinetry for a sleek look.

$10,000 Budget

tonight's menu

mixed green salad
w/herb vinaigrette

roast chicken with
yukon gold potatoes

vanilla
bean ice cream
w/caramel sauce

diy tip

For less than $25, you can add fun and function to your kitchen with a painted-on message board. To make it, brush a section of wall with chalkboard paint and frame it with stock molding.

make your BEST MOVE

Moving one basement door meant more work space for the small kitchen in this Cape Cod house. Then came the fun part.

This kitchen was once an unappetizing vision in pink. But first-time homeowners Sarah Hislop and Dan DeCenzo, a professional carpenter, knew they had the do-it-yourself chops to restyle the space that included pink laminate counters, pink floral wallpaper, linoleum flooring, and worn-out cabinets. Unfortunately, they had to fix the floor plan before they could even take on cosmetic issues. "There wasn't room to cook," says Sarah. "It had awkward flow, minimal counter space, and the appliances desperately needed upgrading."

The first step was to alter the 8×10-foot galley kitchen to add counter space and improve the flow. To get it, the couple relocated the basement door to the adjoining dining room, gaining 4 feet, and allowing them to center the range and create counters on either side of it for cooking ease.

With the structural changes done, the couple could start decorating. They wanted a white, but not all white, kitchen. And they wanted to honor the cottage roots of their home. So they chose a Tiffany-blue and cream palette and covered walls in beaded-board paneling. A mix of open shelving and recessed-panel cabinets turned on the vintage charm for less than $900. The unfinished, stock oak cabinets were primed and painted.

Though Sarah dreamed of oiled soapstone counters, she found a laminate that gave her the look at a fraction of the cost. The tradeoff was worth it when the budget left room for stainless-steel appliances, a vintage farmhouse faucet, and a French door to replace a window for backyard access.

opposite: A single-bowl sink maximizes counter space in this galley kitchen. The couple chose an inexpensive, stainless-steel sink so they could splurge on a sculptural bridge faucet.

Budget Breakdown:

Appliances	$5,000
Sink	$43
Bridge faucet	$425
Cabinets	$850
Hardware	$95
Counters	$200
Lighting	$300
Beaded board	$175
Paint	$100
French door	$800
Total:	**$7,988**

Once the kitchen was opened up, this breakfast room came into focus. New built-in bench seating adds style and storage. Without chair backs, the cushioned benches allow a clear view to the windows.

diy tip

Windows make great doors. When their kitchen didn't have enough light, architecture, or backyard access, this couple enlarged a double-hung window opening in order to fit a single French door.

before

the problem

Bad flow, bad decorating, bad appliances. **the solution:** Relocate a door to the basement stairs to create a longer wall for appliances and counters. Restyle cabinets and surfaces using a save-and-splurge strategy to leave room in the budget for appliances.

budget stretchers

There's no need to sacrifice hard-earned cash to get great style.

Trade cabinets for shelves. Open shelving costs much less than upper cabinets, and it has just as much style and stowing power. To make these shelves more architectural, Dan faced them with 1½-inch pine trim. A friend made the scrolled brackets as a gift.

Save on surfaces. Laminate is the most cost-effective choice for counters. Shop for look-alikes, such as this charcoal gray pattern that mimics pricey soapstone. On the walls, beaded board sold in both sections and sheets is affordable and easy to install.

Put leftovers to good use. The fun details in this kitchen were crafted on the fly using leftover materials. Leftover laminate makes a chic backsplash for the stove, and extra trim was used to make the chalkboard message center.

Don't replace, refinish. Lifting up cracked linoleum revealed 2-inch pine flooring that was in decent shape but needed refinishing, The golden grains weren't what the couple had in mind, so they stained it ebony while they were at it.

Inexpensive inserts. When the budget doesn't make room for custom cabinetry, buy stock and retrofit more function. Wire inserts put in after the fact add accessibility.

Artfully shaped from gleaming materials, a pendant lamp becomes jewelry in a room. An opaque shade directs light onto the table and out of guests' eyes.

1

before

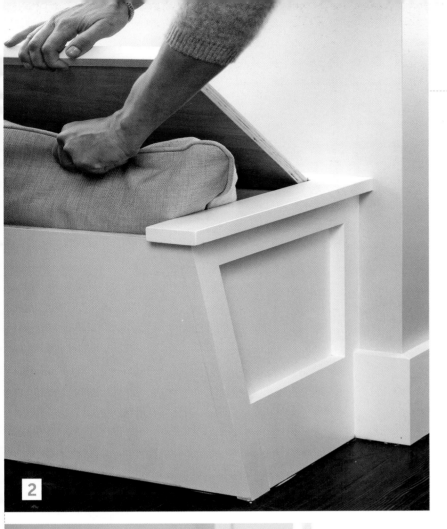

2

3

3 tips for an elegant breakfast nook

An intimate eating enclosure can be as appropriate for family dining as it is gracious entertaining with a scheme that's both easy and elegant.

1. KEEP THE BACKGROUND LIGHT.
Translucent Roman shades set inside the window molding make minimalist coverings in this bank of windows, and accentuate their long, slender shapes. Crisp white trim and sky blue create an airy paint palette that's grounded by dark woods.

2. TUCK AWAY CLUTTER.
Built-in benches with lift-up seats stash decorating materials so they can be changed with the season. The benches themselves are tapered to allow a heel tuck for more comfortable, and demure, seating. A round pedestal table makes sliding in and out of the booth easy.

3. SOFTEN WITH PALE FABRICS.
This space is virtually pattern-free, softened only by neutral fabrics on the toss pillows and seat cushion. Textural embroidery and woven textiles add visual interest to make up for the lack of pattern.

diy tip

Brushed with scrubbable semigloss paint, unfinished beaded board is a thrifty and durable surface for a backsplash. It's sold premilled in strips and panels, making it a doable choice for DIYers.

pouring on
THE CHARM

This cozy Cape Cod has an exterior that makes you say "ahhh."
But inside the side door was a kitchen that evoked a different response.

The outside of this '50s-era Houston house looks *Leave It to Beaver* charming. The kitchen, unfortunately, had been updated in the '80s era of *Family Ties,* with fussy floral fabric, ho-hum appliances, and stale surfaces. For seven years, homeowners Judithe and Les Little lived in a design time warp. "When we moved in, we didn't have any children, so we didn't pay attention to the room," says Judithe. "But every time I'd watch an old show, I felt like they had the same kitchen we did."

Fast-forward a few years and three children, and it was time to refresh the setting. Judithe took her time in the development phase, poring over magazines, catalogs, and websites, and consulting with Les on what they needed and wanted in the space. When it came time to redo the room, the couple decided they could keep a lot that worked for the family, adding signature updates without spending much.

The two rated the layout "just fine." An L-shape stretch of cabinets and appliances surrounding a large island offered enough space for food prep and cleanup. The computer nook and dining area were in the right spots. Even the cupboards could stay with a fresh coat of paint. Construction was limited to installing a beaded-board backplash, new molding, and a range vent. The savings let them to splurge on the stainless-steel, counter-depth pieces and marble counters Judithe found in her search. "I really did my homework and was kind of obsessed," she says, "but in the end I got the kitchen of my dreams."

opposite: Once visually choppy and stylistically dowdy, this kitchen woke up with robin's-egg blue paint and new appliances. Marble counters on the island balance visually (and financially) with butcher block on the rest of the counters.

Budget Breakdown:	
Dishwasher drawers	$1,400
Microwave	$230
Refrigerator	$2,550
Range & back panel	$2,290
Vent	$600
Faucet	$300
Sink	$800
Butcher block	$200
Marble counter	$1,270
Paint & paneling	$300
Lighting	$100
Total:	**$10,040**

The soffit niches stayed,
but now display Judithe's
shapely ironstone servers.
The creamy collectibles add
interest without clutter.

Above the new gas range,
copper pans add gleaming
style and link to the
floor's colors for eye-
appealing balance.

Industrial-chic
stools age the
space as only
vintage pieces
can and share the
same burnished
finish as the
bridge faucet.

the problem

This kitchen's style had grown stale over 30 years, but the layout was efficient. **the solution:** The couple, with the guidance of designer Joetta Moulden, upgraded the appliances and the surfaces.

low cost, high cool

Try these strategies for a better kitchen on a budget.

Preserve the floor plan. Construction dollars went to the details—trim around the refrigerator for a built-in look and a marble countertop.

Read and research. Then read some more. Judithe kept book and magazine images on file, then used the Internet to find deals. She saved hundreds of dollars on the farmhouse sink that way.

Hold back here, go for it there. Spend more on what's important—for Judithe it was new appliances with the hefty look and power of professional pieces.

Keep it simple. Instead of swapping out the doors around the range with glass-front models, the couple decided to just keep them open. As a happy surprise, a microwave fit one shelf perfectly.

Paint is your friend. Pale aqua paint brightened the walls and island and gave the stock beaded-board backsplash style and washability.

6 ways to sneak in extra style

An everyday budget shouldn't stop you from creating a custom design. These ideas can get you started:

1. SPRINKLE WITH FRESH PIECES. A corner desk and farmhouse table work fine for this family, but they swapped tired seating with chic, reproduction French garden seats.

2. PUT EXTRA DOLLARS WHERE THEY COUNT. Sure, it costs a bit more for a marble counter with a double ogee edge, but small custom details elevate a design overall.

3. STRETCH THE BUDGET WITH CREATIVITY. Oak countertops warm this space the right way—with vintage cottage style—but cost much less than most other options.

4. EFFICIENCY COMES WITH REWARDS. Compact and cool dishwasher drawers look slick, make unloading and loading easier, and boast energy efficiency to save both money and resources.

5. THINK OF YOUR FAUCET AS ART. This reproduction farmhouse bridge faucet has a familiarity and a funkiness that play like utilitarian art. Its interesting shape commands attention; its durable construction makes it work like a champ.

6. EDITING COSTS MUCH LESS THAN ADDING. Removing cupboard doors to create open shelves is a low-cost way to break up banks of cabinets. All in white, collectible ironstone and new dinnerware can be both seen—and used.

$10,000 Budget

diy tip

Straightforward changes can give a kitchen an expansive look. Removing kitchen cabinets around the window brought more natural light into the room and increased headroom.

look on the
BRIGHT SIDE

This suburban kitchen needed a brighter outlook—on a budget. So the young homeowners decided to keep the footprint, but give it a major facelift.

The family room in this two-story had the look Rachel Sindelar and husband Brad Penar wanted: bright, inviting, chic. But at the other end of the open space sat a dingy kitchen. "It was so dark and cavelike," she says. "There wasn't enough color and the wood finish on the cabinets was overpowering." Rachel and Brad didn't want an expensive kitchen renovation, so they called on DIY expert Jeni Wright to guide them in updating the kitchen in an affordable yet stylish way.

"The best way to hold costs down is to maintain the original footprint of the room," Wright says. "We just needed to find ways to update surfaces and improve the flow of the space."

The kitchen cabinets were solid, so they stayed but received a fresh coat of white paint. The island was fitted with a cooktop and the stove was removed in favor of a wall oven unit installed next to the pantry. A counter-depth refrigerator increased floor space. This created room for an expanded island, which was remade from the old sink cabinet and two stock cabinets. The curved countertop provided space for young daughters Rosie and Annabelle to snack.

With the addition of the stainless-steel dishwasher, apron sink, and faucet, Rachel was initially worried the room looked too industrial. "But the light, the colors, and the painted cabinetry warmed everything right up—it's not cold or impersonal," she says. Her final verdict on the new look and functionality? "It's awesome."

opposite: The family's budget allowed for two splurge items for Brad, an award-winning brewer: the apron sink and professional-grade faucet. "Even the girls can reach the sink now," Rachel says.

✓ Budget Breakdown:

Apron sink	$470
Faucet	$550
Cabinet hardware	$145
Refrigerator	$1,400
Tile	$700
Dishwasher	$600
Cooktop	$800
Wall oven	$1,250
Lighting	$300
Paint & labor	$2,500
Total:	**$8,715**

before

the problem

This humdrum kitchen didn't have the color and energy of the rest of the house. **the solution:** A pretty patchwork of tile takes the place of dark cabinets on the sink wall and lets in more light for a crisper, brighter design.

island living

Create a custom island with imaginative use of stock cabinets.

Measure the space available. Allow at least 36 inches between the island and the wall cabinets on each side for traffic flow.

Select cabinets to fit space and needs. To include a cooktop, choose a sink base cabinet as the centerpiece. Add a pair of stock cabinets, one on either side, with doors and drawers that offer additional storage.

Screw cabinets together. Build an elevated frame at the back for a serving area if you desire. Trim with molding for a polished finish.

Paint the island. To give your kitchen a furniture look, paint the island a complementary or contrasting color to your cabinets The change of hue makes it appear as an individual piece.

Top with a countertop. Install the counter surface over the cabinets and serving area. If space is tight, add a curve to the serving counter to make it more functional.

diy tip

Paint is your most versatile, colorful ally. A lighthearted paint job can rejuvenate old chairs that have been relegated to basement status. Mix with modern seats and a painted table to spark more personality.

10 DIY Ideas to Steal

YOU CAN UPDATE YOUR KITCHEN WITHOUT TAKING OUT A SECOND MORTGAGE WITH THESE BUDGET-FRIENDLY TIPS.

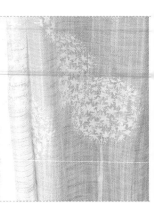

1. Affordable tile

Ceramic tile is a classic kitchen treatment. The luxe look is surprisingly inexpensive, too, if you search for bargains. Look at home centers or check the collections of favorite tile designers. Wright selected five colors from Ann Sacks' line.

2 Shop for guidance

Certified kitchen designers who know product lines inside and out often staff kitchen sales areas and design desks at home centers. Their services are free for customers.

3. Subtle stencil

With so much color introduced at the dining table, the curtains at the sliding glass doors needed to stay neutral to avoid competing focal points. Plain linen draperies would have fit the bill, but Wright decided to add some subtle visual interest with a tone-on-tone stencil in a botanical motif. Use fabric paint to keep your curtains washable.

4. Make it sparkle

Spray paint makes updating old furnishings a snap with the dizzying variety of paint finishes and colors available for all types of surfaces. Wright used metallic chrome paint to give old cafeteria chairs a new lease on life. The brushed metal look links the chairs to the stainless-steel kitchen appliances.

5 Paint chip artwork

Paper collages on the pantry wall reiterate the colorful palette throughout the kitchen. Wright created these delightful bird portraits using color chips from the paint store. To make, find an online clip art design as your guide. Cut and place color chips to fill in your design. Secure with glue when you're satisfied with the placement. With a sewing machine, sew a running stitch randomly over the finished collage and frame.

9. Stainless for less

If you want the look of stainless-steel appliances but your budget isn't friendly to the idea of a new purchase and your existing appliances are still in good working order, don't give up. You can have your new look at rock-bottom prices with a liquid stainless-steel kit. Shop for a water-base, paint-on solution that gives you a 100 percent stainless-steel coating in three easy steps.

String along

Make your own globe lamp! Blow up a 36-inch balloon (at party supply stores) to about 30 inches. Paint the balloon with fabric stiffener and wrap with crochet string dipped in the stiffener. Apply additional stiffener as necessary. Let dry for 24 hours, then pop the balloon. Cut a slit in a butter tub lid; insert light fixture. Tie a knot in the wire under the lid to keep the bulb unit in place. Cut a hole in the top of the globe; feed fixture and lid through the hole, folding the lid as necessary.

6. Give 'em the boot

Turn everyday objects into charming table accents. Unused children's rubber boots become flower vases with a spray coat of bubblegum pink paint in a matte finish. Insert a slim cylinder vase into the boot top to keep flowers fresh. Set your playful accent on a pretty pink embroidered placemat. Wright pulled the color from the vibrant rug under the table.

10

7. Make a shelf

Unadorned, nickel-plated shelf brackets make it a budget-friendly breeze to install open shelving. Available online or cut to the desired width from your own material, the shelf slides into a bracket on each end, which conceals the cut edge.

8. Curve it

The narrow serving area of the island did little more than collect clutter. A generous curve on the new countertop increases serving space without widening the island's footprint.

how to:
paint cabinets

New brushed-nickel hardware links to stainless-steel appliances and adds a modern finishing touch.

Materials:
_Liquid sandpaper
_¼-inch nap paint roller
_Primer
_220-grit sandpaper
_Tack cloth
_Paintbrush, roller, or sprayer
_Paint

DIY paint tips

Start by **cleaning cabinets with a strong detergent** to remove surface oils and grime.

Applying a high-grade primer is the secret to giving your cabinet finish a good foundation. Look for **water-base primers that will adhere to any type of surface**, including wood, plastic, and laminate.

Look for **quality latex paint that is formulated for kitchen cabinetry**. These paints dry extra hard, which prevents doors from sticking to the cabinet frame.

What they did...
It's a shame to replace solid cabinetry just because the color isn't right for you. That's where paint comes in. Paint was the key to lightening and brightening this family kitchen on a budget. With their savings, Rachel and Brad invested in a stainless-steel apron sink and a professional-grade faucet.

step 1

Prime your surface. Wipe the cabinet surface with liquid sandpaper, or use a fine grade of sandpaper to lightly scuff the surface. Using a ¼-inch nap roller or paintbrush, apply primer. Let dry.

step 2

Sand lightly. Sand the primed surface with 220-grit sandpaper for better paint adherence. Wipe thoroughly with a tack cloth.

step 3

Apply the paint. Brush, roll, or spray the cabinet surface with paint. Let dry. Spraying on paint will result in the smoothest finish, but all doors will have to be removed for painting.

step 4

Finish with a second coat. For even coverage, apply a second coat of paint.

angled brush
The best tool for painting areas where you need control. Hold this brush like a pencil.

mini roller
Mini rollers make it easy to paint small areas and are ideal for getting into tight corners.

paint pad
Ideal for a clean line, particularly in hard-to-reach spaces and corners where rollers won't fit.

trim guide
Try this tool when painting trim edges against walls.

diy tip

For smooth coverage sans brush and roller strokes, consider using a paint sprayer. Not just for paint pros anymore, residential-grade sprayers cover faster and more evenly than other applicators.

how to
reinvent
your cabinets

When you need big change on a small budget, go for impact. Try one of these 10 doable ideas for updating your cabinets, and watch your whole kitchen spring to life.

Cover the wood in two coats of teal paint. Position a monogram sticker (available at crafts shops) on the cabinet door; use a scraper to press evenly over the sticker and wood. Carefully remove the backing paper, then add a border in a smaller-scale design.

Base-coat the cabinet with white paint. Spray stencil adhesive on a medallion-style stencil. Center the stencil on the cabinet door, pressing firmly. Use a stencil brush to pounce aqua paint all over the design, removing the stencil when covered.

cabinet couture
tile with style

If you have some tiling experience, try this clever idea: When starting with new cabinets, order them unpainted and designed with wood-frame, "prepped for glass" doors. Delete the preinstalled glass from the order to receive doors with empty centers. Or order replacement doors online and click on "frame-only doors." (Consult a hardware store for sturdy hinges.) Next, cut a piece of plywood to the size of the opening on the back of the door, less $1/8$ inch around the perimeter. Using tile mastic, set tiles onto the board, working from the center out. The outermost tiles will need to be cut to fit. Place the tiled panel into the door frame using panel clips that come with your door (no adhesive needed).

Spray the cabinet black (use two coats if necessary). Cut cork adhesive paper to fit the door panel. Peel off the paper backing and adhere the cork. Tip: This idea works best on cabinets made of soft wood such as pine.

Blast the cabinet with green spray paint. When dry, tape off the door panel with quick-release painter's tape. Spray the panel with chalkboard paint, then remove the painter's tape.

old-world cool
Wedgwood style

Using traditional Wedgwood pottery as inspiration, paint the cabinet fronts cornflower blue, then add wood gingerbread appliqués from a crafts shop. DIY tip: Apply glaze (this is burnt umber) to give new paint jobs a vintage patina. Paint cabinets with semigloss acrylic paint (we used two coats). Using wood glue, adhere cream-painted cutouts to the corners and center of the cabinet door. Using an old brush, apply water-base glaze over the entire cabinet surface. Rub the glaze with a rag, working it in to create the desired effect.

Remove the door panel by drilling a $\frac{1}{2}$-inch hole in the center of the panel, inserting a jigsaw, then cutting an X from corner to corner. Shake the door to remove the loose pieces. Paint the frame brown, then glue a bamboo table runner, cut to size, behind the frame.

Remove the door panel and add a thin plywood base, as shown in "Tile with Style," *page 175*. Paint the cabinet white. Cut tin ceiling panels to fit the frame. Paint the panel a soft color, such as this celery green. When dry, glue the panel to the wood base.

cabinet coverups
spice is nice

Instead of tiling a backsplash, keep this fun dot pattern at eye level by tiling the centers of cabinet doors. DIY tip: Speed the tiling process by using premixed mastic and a grout that is sold in a tube and spreads like glue. Paint or stain the cabinet to complement the tile design. Center your tile design on the cabinet door. Apply mastic to the wood, then adhere the tiles. Let the mastic dry following the manufacturer's directions, then grout the tile. Finish the outside tile edges with picture molding painted white. Use wood glue to affix the molding.

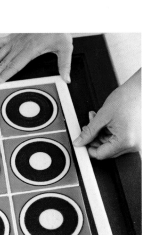

radiate style
screen star

Home improvment and hardware stores are packed with creative materials to freshen your cabinets. Case in point: A metal radiator screen, available in varying sizes, colors, and styles, gives a basic cabinet an interesting look—for very little cash. DIY tip: Once you remove a cabinet door's center panel, you have plenty of replacement possibilities, including glass, metal, fabric, and beaded board. We like the modern industrial look this black screen conjures up. To do it, first remove the center panel and paint the cabinet white. Glue 1-inch-wide wood strips, painted black, on the back of the door frame so only ½ inch shows from the front. Use tin snips to cut the radiator screen to fit the cabinet frame. Squeeze a bead of wood glue on each wood strip, then position the screen on top.

DIY kitchen
planning guide

Upgrading your kitchen makes sense for many reasons. See how a few changes can benefit the environment, your family's health, and your wallet.

Like a box of favorite recipes, a kitchen remodel is full of possibilities. The process can smooth an awkward layout, refresh dated decor, and replace inefficient appliances. And even if you move away, your efforts might produce a higher price or a quicker sale.

Let us spark your ideas and help you set your goals. Need more inspiration? Tour model homes and showrooms. Scan design books, blogs, and websites.

But start with the reality of your existing kitchen—what you like and what you don't. Ask others in your family, especially other cooks, what works and what doesn't in the floor plan, traffic flow, storage, and equipment. Ask them how it feels when you entertain or just hang out there.

Create a tentative budget and a wish list, knowing you probably can't have it all. Even the smallest detail—a display shelf for honeymoon souvenirs, a sports drink dispenser in the refrigerator—can help lead your kitchen designer, architect, or contractor to your dream kitchen.

Everything starts with a thoughtful layout and well-chosen appliances, sinks, faucets, countertops, and cabinetry. Within those options, think "green." Whether you want to lower your utility bills, create a healthier home, or protect the environment, ecologically sound and energy-efficient products, materials, and strategies turn remodeling into renewal.

planning the space

As you consider how best to use your space, it helps to know the recommended measurements and clearances that make a kitchen safe, functional, and comfortable. With these in hand, visit showrooms to see the guidelines in action.

EXPERT ADVICE—FREE!

The National Kitchen and Bath Association's free *Kitchen & Bath Workbook* guides you through a project step by step. A worksheet and sketching space help you prep for in-person time with a designer. Order your copy at *nkba.org* in the Kitchen & Bath Tools section.

stats to study

BAR COUNTER
Height: 28–45 inches
Knee space: 12–18 inches
Base-cabinet height: 34 inches

COOKTOP CLEARANCE
24 inches above (30 inches if surface above is unprotected)

COUNTER HEIGHT
Standard: 36 inches
Maximum: 45 inches

COUNTERTOP CLEARANCE
15 inches to cabinets above

COUNTERTOP DEPTH
24 inches

FOOD-PREP AREA
36-inch-wide work surface for each cook (adjacent to water source)

SINK
If a kitchen has only one, locate close to or across from cooking surface or refrigerator

COUNTER SPACE
Primary sink: 24 inches on dishwasher side; 18 inches on the other side
Secondary sink: 18 inches on one side

REFRIGERATOR COUNTER SPACE
15-inch space within 48 inches on handle side

DISHWASHER
No more than 36 inches from sink

MICROWAVE
Locate bottom 3 inches below user's shoulder but no more than 54 inches above floor (place undercounter microwave bottom at least 15 inches above floor)

MICROWAVE COUNTER SPACE
15-inch space above, below, or on handle side

OVEN COUNTER SPACE
15-inch space above or adjacent, or on an island or peninsula no more than 48 inches away

WALKWAY WIDTHS
36 inches (work area on one side only)

WORK AISLE WIDTHS
One cook: 42 inches
Two cooks: 48 inches

WORK TRIANGLE
Include at least one and ensure that no major traffic pattern runs through it

Meaurements are suggested minimums unless otherwise noted. These recommendations were adapted from guidelines of the National Kitchen and Bath Association (NKBA). For more information, or to find a certified kitchen designer (CKD), visit nkba.org; call 800/843-6522; or write NKBA, 687 Willow Grove St., Hackettstown, NJ 07840.

choosing appliances

Efficient and convenient, modern appliances save time and steps—and run so quietly that you can enjoy your kitchen as a living space. Energy-efficient models also save you money and help save the environment.

cooking

RANGES Most traditional ranges—with four burners above and an oven below—are 30 inches wide, but 24- and 36-inch models are also available. Commercial-style models, 48 or 60 inches wide, accommodate six burners or a combination of burners and griddle or grill. Gas or electric ranges can be freestanding (with finished side panels) or made to slide between cabinets. Some models boast two ovens or a built-in warming drawer. Bakers often prefer the even heat of electricity, which has led to dual-fuel ranges that top an electric oven with gas burners.

OVENS Built into a wall or under a counter, 30- or 36-inch-wide ovens offer thermal or convection (or combination) cooking in single or double cavities. Built-in speed-cook ovens typically combine convection, microwave, and sometimes steam functions.

MICROWAVES These come in countertop, built-in, over-the-range, and drawer models.

COOKTOPS Some cooks swear by the instant control of gas. Others prefer electric coils, or they select radiant, halogen, or induction elements under ceramic-glass surfaces. Electric cooktops now offer rapid-cycle elements that fine-tune the heat setting as precisely as gas. Modular cooktops let you assemble functions you like best from burners, grills, griddles, woks, steamers, and more. Diner-style flat-top cookers sear, sauté, and stir-fry directly on a steel surface.

RANGE HOODS Wall-mount, undercabinet, ceiling-mount, and downdraft models come in widths and exhaust capabilities to match any range or cooktop's output of heat, steam, and grease. Compare ratings—lower means quieter—to find the power you need at the sound level you prefer.

cleaning

FULL-SIZE DISHWASHERS Standard models 18–30 inches wide are usually built in under the countertop, where they can be disguised by cabinet trim panels. Capacities range from 10 to 16 place settings, and wash cycles vary from three to 12. Some include a steam cycle for stuck-on food.

DISHWASHER DRAWERS These are about half the size of a standard dishwasher—and use half the energy, water, and detergent. They can be stacked in pairs or installed singly. Load one with delicate crystal and the other with greasy cookware, or separate dishes to follow kosher dietary laws. Some drawer models also offer heating elements and water softeners.

cooling

FREESTANDING VS. BUILT-IN
Standard refrigerators measure 27–32 inches deep, so they stand out from standard 24-inch-deep base cabinets. More expensive 24-inch-deep built-ins fit flush with cabinets (and, with trim panels, almost disappear). Pro-style models sport stainless-steel frames with glass doors. Retro or European styling adds curvy doors and colorful finishes. Full-size all-freezer and all-refrigerator units are another built-in variation for a custom kitchen.

FREEZER POSITION Units with top-mount and bottom-mount freezers are 24–36 inches wide, with a capacity of 10 to almost 28 cubic feet. Bottom-mount units cost more for the same capacity but are more energy-efficient, and most homeowners find having fresh food on top more user-friendly. Side-by-side units are split vertically, with frozen food on the left and fresh on the right. Most are 30–36 inches wide, with capacities of 10–29 cubic feet; pro-style models measure up to 72 inches wide and 48 cubic feet. Narrower sections make bulky items difficult to store. When open, the slender doors occupy less floor space but can block countertop access on both sides.

FRENCH-DOOR These armoire-style models store fresh food behind twin doors at eye level and frozen food behind a door or in a drawer below. They're 30–42 inches wide and 18–20 cubic feet. Freestanding and built-in styles also offer counter-depth versions for a built-in look.

UNDERCOUNTER Ideal for small kitchens, these refrigerators are 15–24 inches wide (most at counter depth) with up to 3.9-cubic-foot capacity. Use one for produce at the prep sink or for snacks and beverages near the family room.

DRAWER A new solution for tricky layouts, refrigerator or freezer drawers install under a counter, in a wall, or in an island. Models range from 15 to 36 inches wide and 3.9–6.7 cubic feet.

specialty

ICEMAKERS Undercounter icemakers 15–24 inches wide produce up to 60 pounds of ice per day, and they store up to 35 pounds. Some require a gravity drain or drain pump, but others need only a water line.

WINE AND BEVERAGE REFRIGERATORS Wine storage units, ranging from 15-inch-wide undercounter models to 30x84-inch freestanding units, hold 25–150 wine bottles at electronically monitored temperatures, from 43°F to 65°F. High-end models offer up to three storage zones, tinted-glass doors, and pullout shelves tilted to keep corks moist. For less-sensitive drinks, undercounter chillers store cans and bottles outside your work core, freeing your refrigerator for other items.

WARMING DRAWERS Cooked dishes suffer when they wait for family members to come home or for guests to finish their salads. Warming drawers 24–36 inches wide make sense installed near your range or wall oven. With a range of 82°F to 250°F, drawers warm plates, proof bread dough, or keep soup hot. Moisture controls help food retain a moist or crisp texture.

going green

Old appliances are energy hogs, especially refrigerators. According to the Department of Energy, new models consume about half the electricity of 1993 refrigerators. Energy Star labeling (energystar.gov) highlights which dishwashers and refrigerators are most efficient.

REFRIGERATORS Side-by-side models use 10 percent more electricity than top-freezer models. Through-the-door ice-and-water dispensers and automatic icemakers increase electricity use by up to 20 percent. Mostly full refrigerators and freezers run less often.

DISHWASHERS Run them only when full; drawer models are ideal for small loads. Today's dishwashers use less than half the water and one-fourth the power of 10-year-old models. No-heat drying draws less energy but takes longer to finish the job. Delayed-start washing takes advantage of low overnight utility rates.

choosing sinks & faucets

From a restaurant-style steel basin and spray head to a rustic farm sink with nostalgic copper tap, there's a sink-and-faucet team for any decor or cooking style. Two sinks are better than one if your household has several cooks or if you entertain often. New faucets offer convenient operation, flashy finishes, and water-saving mechanisms.

sinks

MATERIALS

Acrylic, composite, or solid-surfacing: Molded-through color hides chips and scratches. Synthetic material offers a stone look with less weight and easier installation.

Enameled steel or cast iron: Enameled steel might chip; enameled cast iron is heavy but more durable. Both come in many colors.

Stainless steel: This popular material teams well with stainless-steel appliances. For durability, check the gauge: Lower means thicker.

Stone: Heavy slate, soapstone, granite, and concrete offer organic chic but are costly to buy and install. The surface is unforgiving of dropped plates and glasses.

CONFIGURATIONS

Standard: This 33×22-inch format contains two bowls of equal or nearly equal size. Optional extra-deep bowls (10–14 inches) accommodate tall pots and pans.

Large single-bowl: Typically 25×22 inches, this type uses less counter space but still welcomes large pans. Farm, or apron-front, sinks are a stylish version.

Three-bowl: With extra options in depth and proportion, this style has a third, shallow bowl for food preparation.

Modular: Designed for undermount installation, individual bowls come in several shapes and sizes. You create your ideal arrangement.

Bar or prep: Favorites for islands, these secondary basins come in geometric or free-form shapes.

Corner: This sink's shortened L shape optimizes counter space.

faucets

SINGLE-HOLE OR POST-MOUNT
Only one hole pierces the sink deck or countertop, conserving space.

POT FILLER
This spigot, mounted on a counter or wall near a range or cooktop, makes filling large pots easier.

PRERINSE
Adapted from restaurant kitchens, this style boasts a tall, flexible spray hose that reaches any sink corner.

WALL-MOUNT
Plumbed through the wall behind and above the sink, this type can look vintage or contemporary.

BRIDGE
An exposed channel links handles and spout.

GOOSENECK OR HIGH-ARC
This tall, arched spout eases filling large or deep pots and tall vases.

PULLOUT FAUCET
A two-piece spout functions as both a faucet and a retractable sprayer.

going healthy

Have your water tested for lead, chemicals, and other contaminants. If tests show your water is unsafe, install undersink, separate-tap, or faucet-equipped filters.

choosing countertops

Practical countertops must meet your needs and fit your decor. It's OK to mix materials—for instance, stone for an island where guests gather and laminate at the kids' snack-and-homework zone. When comparing prices, consider longevity and maintenance. Also note whether each material is priced by the linear or square foot.

materials

BAMBOO This renewable grass can be assembled using food-safe adhesives.

BUTCHER BLOCK Made from laminated wood, this is best for baking areas and island tops. Seal with oil to boost moisture resistance; let knife marks create a patina, or sand the surface smooth.

CONCRETE Cast in place or installed as preformed slabs, sealed concrete resists burns, stains, and scratches but is labor-intensive to install. Customize it with tints, texture, or inset shells, glass, or other items.

GLASS Sleek and dramatic, tempered glass comes in clear or translucent forms with a smooth or textured surface. Recycled composite glass is also an option. Glass is waterproof and heat-tolerant; use a cutting board to avoid scratches.

GRANITE Today's most popular choice offers a variety of colors and patterns. Shopping at a stoneyard costs more than ordering from a sample but lets you buy the exact

piece you want. Reduce cost by using granite tiles or remnants instead of a single slab. Granite is durable and impervious to heat but requires professional installation and periodic sealing to repel stains.

LAMINATE Affordable laminate comes off-the-rack as a one-piece counter and backsplash in limited color choices. Or if you custom-order from a home center or kitchen dealer, you'll find hundreds of colors and patterns, some that mimic stone, metal, or wood. Customize your project with a shaped edge or textured finish. The material is easy to install but has visible seams. Use a cutting board for slicing and trivets for hot pans.

MARBLE AND LIMESTONE These stones are classic and luxurious, but they're softer and more porous than granite, so they are more likely to scratch or stain.

QUARTZ-SURFACING Also called engineered stone, this blend of ground quartz, resins, and pigments produces consistent stonelike patterns. It is nonporous and heat- and scratch-resistant.

SOAPSTONE Soft and silky, soapstone chips more easily than granite. Like other stones, it resists heat. Treat it with mineral oil to repel moisture.

SOLID-SURFACING Look for panels and veneers made of plastic resins in many colors

and patterns. The nonporous material resists stains; scratches can be sanded out. Solid-surfacing sinks create a seamless installation.

STAINLESS STEEL Sanitary and stainproof, this surface complements a stainless-steel sink and perfects a pro-style kitchen. Steel is heatproof and waterproof, but a shiny finish can show scratches and fingerprints. Ready-made sections fit standard counter sizes; custom installations fit others.

TILE Glazed ceramic or porcelain tiles in many shapes, colors, and sizes are water- and heat-resistant. If they chip, they're easy to replace. You might need to regrout every few years.

going green

Earth-friendly countertop materials are easily extracted and manufactured. Now it's easy to find surfaces with reclaimed or recycled content:

CERAMIC OR PORCELAIN TILES Made from plentiful clay, they can contain recycled glass and ceramics. Avoid lead-base glazes.

COMPOSITES Solid-surfacing, engineered quartz, and glass aggregate surround plastic, stone, and glass in a resin or cement base.

PAPER COMPOSITES These contain recycled paper and other fibers impregnated with resin for heat and stain resistance.

RECYCLED ALUMINUM These tiles and panels use industrial scraps.

choosing cabinets

Taking up about 40 percent of most kitchen renovation budgets, cabinetry represents a long-term investment. But cabinets also anchor a room's style and store items from couscous to cookie sheets. Shop cabinet materials and construction wisely.

construction types

STOCK Sold ready-to-install at home centers and dealers or ready-to-assemble online, stock cabinets are standing inventory. Your dealer might not have every unit in stock, but special orders take as little as a week. Stock cabinets range from 6 to 42 inches wide, in 3-inch increments. This is the most affordable option.

SEMICUSTOM Next up in price, semicustom cabinetry is also factory-made in standard sizes, but you'll find more woods, finishes, and decorative features. Widths measure up to 60 inches. Options include pantry units, sliding shelves, and drawer inserts. Allow four to six weeks for semicustom orders.

CUSTOM With the most options to offer, custom cabinetry is designed, built, and installed to fit your space. A professional kitchen designer can help you establish an efficient layout. Exotic woods, ornate details, and period styles add cost and delivery time but result in a one-of-a-kind kitchen.

To get the best cabinets within your budget, choose a compact work area and standard sizes. Consider mixing a few custom pieces and accessories with semicustom or stock units.

INFO GATHERING

Collect cabinet manufacturer catalogs, books, and magazine photos that appeal to you. Show these to your kitchen designer or showroom staff as examples of the overall style you're after.

FACE FRAME In this traditional-look construction, a solid-wood frame attaches to the front of the cabinet box. Hinges, hidden or visible, attach the door to the frame. Because the frame overlaps the door opening, drawers must be slightly narrower than the cabinet box.

FRAMELESS This more contemporary-look construction creates slightly more capacity. When the door is open, you see the ends of the box panels. Door hinges mount inside the cabinet, so they're hidden when doors are closed.

door and drawer frames

FULL OVERLAY
Doors cover the face frame—or the entire box front on frameless cabinets—leaving minimal space between doors and drawers.

PARTIAL OVERLAY
Doors cover the frame by about ½ inch; the rest of the frame shows around the door.

INSET
Doors and drawer fronts install flush with the face frame. The precision of this design is most often seen in custom cabinetry.

DOOR DESIGNS Slab doors are flat and sleek. Paneled doors range from mitered squares to gentle arches or fancier cathedral tops. Inserts are raised or recessed; some are accented with beaded board or decorative molding. Use glass, bamboo, wire, or paper instead of wood to add more personality.

EMBELLISHMENTS Millwork and architectural detail give cabinets custom character. Use decorative brackets called corbels under a shelf or a wooden range hood. Bun feet and turned legs also enhance cabinets' furniture styling. Crown, dentil, or rope molding looks rich and covers blemishes and joints.

SIGNS OF QUALITY Solid wood is beautiful for cabinet fronts, but most back, side, and bottom panels are now made from plywood, particleboard, or medium-density fiberboard. Don't worry. These engineered woods are more stable than solid wood in changing humidity—especially useful for a sink base unit. For additional durability, metal-frame cabinetry is another option.

When comparing cabinets, look for these quality indicators: Drawers should have solid-wood or plywood sides with rabbeted, doweled, or dovetailed joints. Self-closing drawers and tray glides should support 75–100 pounds when extended. In wall cabinets, adjustable shelves add flexibility.

A blue-and-white "Certified Cabinet" seal from the Kitchen Cabinet Manufacturers Association shows that a cabinet has met industry guidelines for durable construction.

STORAGE ACCESSORIES To make the most of every inch of storage, shop accessory options. Store cookware on pullout shelves or wire organizers. Angled corner drawers put potentially wasted space to work. Pullout pantry and spice storage makes canned and dry goods more accessible.

WOODS AND FINISHES Natural wood offers a selection of colors and grains. Oak, pine, and hickory have prominent grain patterns and suit traditional or country styles. Maple, cherry, and mahogany look classic or contemporary depending on the finish.

Stain affects wood color but shows its grain, while paint creates a solid finish that hides grain. In general, pick a richer or darker finish for a traditional look and a light, natural finish for a modern mood.

going green

Green cabinet materials include bamboo, formaldehyde-free medium-density fiberboard, wheatboard or strawboard, and plywoods and veneers certified by the Forest Stewardship Council. For healthy indoor air, choose water-base, low-VOC finishes applied before cabinets reach your home.

editors' favorite resources

The sources for kitchen products are endless, here are a few of the favorites used in the kitchens in this book.

appliances

BOSCH
bosch-home.com; 248/876-1000

FRIGIDAIRE
Frigidaire.com; 800/374-4432

GENERAL ELECTRIC
geappliances.com; 800/626-2005

KENMORE
Kenmore.com; 888/536-6673

KITCHENAID
kitchenaid.com; 800/422-1230

LG ELECTRONICS
lg.com; 800/243-0000

MAYTAG
maytag.com; 800/344-1274

SUB-ZERO/WOLF
subzero.com; 800/222-7820

VIKING
vikingrange.com; 888/845-4641

WHIRLPOOL
whirlpool.com; 866/698-2538

cabinetry

ARMSTRONG
Armstrong.com; 800/228-1804

IKEA
ikea.com

KRAFTMAID
kraftmaid.com; 888/562-7744

MASTERBRAND
masterbrand.com; 812/482-2527

THOMASVILLE
thomasvillecabinetry.com

tile

AMERICAN OLEAN
americanolean.com; 888/268-8153

ANN SACKS
annsacks.com; 800/278-8453

ARMSTRONG
armstrong.com; 800/233-3823

CROSSVILLE
crossvilleinc.com; 931/484-4248

WALKER ZANGER
walkerzanger.com; 713/880-9292

countertops

DUPONT (CORIAN)
Dupont.com; 800/426-7466

GREEN MOUNTAIN SOAPSTONE
greenmountainsoapstone.com; 800/585-5636

FORMICA
formica.com; 800/367-6422

SILESTONE
silestone.com; 800/291-1311

WILSONART
wilsonart.com; 800/433-3222

hardware

AMEROCK
amerock.com

HICKORY HARDWARE
hickoryhardware.com; 877/556-2918

KOHLER
kohler.com; 800/456-4537

primers and paints

BEHR
Behr.com; 800/854-0133

BENJAMIN MOORE
Benjaminmoore.com; 800/672-4686

DUNN-EDWARDS PAINTS
Dunnedwards.com; 888/337-2468

DUTCH BOY
Dutchboy.com; 800/828-5669

FARROW & BALL
Farrow-ball.com; 888/511-1121

GLIDDEN
Glidden.com; 800/454-3336

KILZ
Kilz.com; 800/325-3552

MARTHA STEWART SIGNATURE COLOR THROUGH SHERWIN-WILLIAMS
Sherwin-williams.com; 800/474-3794

OLYMPIC
Olympic.com; 800/441-9695

PITTSBURGH PAINT
Ppgpittsburghpaints.com; 800/441-9695

PRATT& LAMBERT
Prattandlambert.com; 800/289-7728

SHERWIN-WILLIAMS
Sherwin-williams.com; 800/474-3794

VALSPAR
Valspar.com; 800/845-9061

index